Acknowledgments

The authors are deeply grateful to all of the Deans of Admission and college counselors who contributed their time, insights, and suggestions to this project. For making this book possible (quite literally), special thanks to the following successful college applicants who contributed their *great* admission essays:

Nathaniel August *65, 99*
Rachel Becker *92*
Angel Brownawell *96*
Stephen A. Byers *36*
Michelle Cavanaugh *75*
Carrie Cook *63*
Stacy Cowley *55, 88*
Gregory DeFelice *98*
Vincent Duron *94*
Samvid Dwarakanath *69*
Mike Epstein *108*
Andrew Farris *77*
Sarah Hannah Felix *50*
Adam Feltcher *58*
Aaron Michael Feuer *46*
Amy Goldberg *76*
Cheryl Greenspoon *84*
Isaac Husain *39*
Lara Kammrath *81*
Rachel Kester *52*
Nick Klingensmith *34*
Shari LaGrotte *62*
Vicky Law *48*

Nicholas Lehmann *54*
Laura Leichum *47*
Jean Leng *103*
Ari Levy *73, 90*
Robert Luo *43*
Joshua Newman *87*
Linda Pan *60*
Benjamin Eric Peterson *85*
Jonathan Putman *79*
Jessica Roake *105*
Nathaniel Rolnick *41, 93*
Kendell St. Brigid *40*
William Sokol *37*
Mandy Sonenshine *71*
Cindy Stanwyck *83*
Tina Tahmassebi *67*
Pei-Hsin (Michelle) Tsai *53*
Seth Weinert *67*
Holly Wilkie *44*
Ryan Wilsey *78*
Adam Winter *101*
Judy Yeh *104*

Additional acknowledgments by Cynthia Muchnick:

> I am grateful to my mentor James Montoya, formerly the Dean of Admission at Stanford University, now Vice President for the College Board, for steering me toward the admission field; Ted O'Neill, Dean of Admission at the University of Chicago, for the opportunity to pursue it; Helen Britt, my college counselor and now

colleague, formerly with the Branson School; Vicky De Felice of Salter, De Felice and Geller for her resourceful essay collecting and advice; Linda Winrow at the University School in Ft. Lauderdale, Florida; Nelie McNeal at the Francis Parker School in San Diego, California; A.J. Aucamp at St. Andrews in Boca Raton, Florida; and Susan Paton at the Hopkins School in New Haven, Connecticut. Finally, I could not thrive in my work without the constant love and support of my husband Adam.

About the Authors

Mark Alan Stewart has written numerous admission guides for high school and college students, including *Perfect Personal Statements— Law, Business, Medical, and Graduate School* (Peterson's, ARCO). He brings to this book more than a decade of experience as a college and law school instructor and student advisor. Mr. Stewart's other Peterson's (ARCO) publications for college and graduate school admission include:

30 Days to the LSAT
30 Days to the GMAT
Words for Smart Test Takers
Math for Smart test Takers
GRE-LSAT Logic Workbook
GRE-LSAT-GMAT-MCAT Reading Comprehension Workbook
GMAT CAT-Answers to the Real Essay Questions
GRE-Answers to the Real Essay Questions

Cynthia Clumeck Muchnick is a graduate of Stanford University, where she worked as a campus tour guide and volunteer student coordinator in recruiting admitted students for the Office of Undergraduate Admission. Since then, Ms. Muchnick has served as an Assistant Director of Undergraduate Admission at the Illinois Institute of Technology and at the University of Chicago. She has taught high school history as well as numerous essay writing workshops. *Best College Admission Essays* is Ms. Muchnick's third Peterson's publication.

Contents

PART 3

ADVICE FROM THE EXPERTS 113

PART 1

Insights on Essays

The fact that you're reading this book means one of two things:

1. a school counselor has warned you that the essay "can play a significant role in the admission decision, and so you'd better take it seriously"

2. a friend who is already working on his or her essays has suggested that you "go buy one of those books that includes a bunch of essays to get some ideas"

Both the counselor and the friend are right, but you're probably still worried about all of this—for one (or more) of three reasons:

1. your GPA isn't spectacular, and you doubt that even a great essay will get you into your first-choice college

2. you don't consider yourself a "good" writer or a "creative" writer

3. you believe you've lived such an ordinary life that you have nothing interesting, important, or unique to say to the admission committee

Wrong, wrong, and wrong! Okay, there's nothing you can do about your GPA (except to improve your grades in the future). Let's concentrate on what you *can* do. So you're not another Hemingway or Twain. Does this mean you have to settle for a college admission essay that is just "okay"

or even "pretty good"? Absolutely not. Writing effective essays does not require creative genius, divine inspiration, or a high I.Q. It does not require that you've traveled, volunteered to further social causes, dined with well-known influential people, or looked death in the face. All it requires is some self-knowledge, time, and effort.

Part 1 of this book is crammed with practical, useful tools to help you generate ideas and craft a masterpiece. Don't feel, however, that you have to follow every piece of advice included here. These tips are meant to help you get started; they are not intended as hard-and-fast rules for writing admission essays.

Before the brainstorming begins, let's look at the essay topics and questions themselves and at the evaluation process.

COMMON ESSAY TOPICS AND QUESTIONS

The majority of essay topics appearing on college applications look very similar to the four topics included in the Common Application, a standard application form sponsored by the National Association of Secondary School Principals (NASSP). The Common Application simplifies and streamlines the application process. It is currently accepted by about 230 colleges and universities. The Personal Statement section of the Common Application reads as follows:

> This personal statement helps us become acquainted with you as an individual in ways different from courses, grades, test scores, and other objective data. It will demonstrate your ability to organize thoughts to express yourself. We are looking for an essay that will help us know you better as a person and as a student. Please write an essay (250-500 words) on a topic of your choice or on one of the options listed below. You may attach your essay on separate sheets (same size, please).
>
> 1. Evaluate a significant experience or achievement that has special meaning to you.
>
> 2. Discuss some issue of personal, local, or national concern and its importance to you.

3. Indicate a person who has had a significant influence on you, and describe that influence.*

4. Describe a fictional character, an historical figure, or a creative work in art, music, science, etc. that has had an influence on you, and explain that influence.

5. Topic of your choice

Even among the schools that don't use the Common Application, some variation on one or more of these four topics is often used. Nevertheless, a wide variety of additional essay topics and questions also appear on college applications. The essay topics vary so widely that it would be futile to try to list them all or to categorize them here. Besides, there is no best way to respond to specific types of questions and topics (regardless of what you might read elsewhere). The key is to follow general guidelines and to discover your own style and voice that you can apply to any kind of essay. You can find The Common Application in the "Research" area of the NASSP Web site at www.nassp.org.

THE ROLE OF THE ESSAY IN THE ADMISSION PROCESS

✎ HOW IMPORTANT IS MY ESSAY IN THE ADMISSION DECISION?

It depends. Except at the most selective schools, if your GPA and SAT scores are both remarkably high, then as long as you don't write something patently stupid or offensive in your essays, your GPA and SAT scores will probably convince the admission committee at the school to admit you. On the other hand, if a particular school is a long-shot for you, then even a great essay will probably not in itself persuade the admission committee to admit you. The fact is: the closer you are to the borderline, the more significant a role your essay will play in the admission decision.

---

* © 2001, Common Application Group. Used with permission.

✎ CAN I BE ASSURED THAT SOMEONE AT THE COLLEGE WILL READ MY ESSAY(S)?

Most colleges will tell you essentially: "Assuming that you have submitted a complete application and have met our application deadline, your essay(s) will be read by at least one person in our office." Generally speaking, this is true. However, smaller schools—especially private liberal arts colleges—with small applicant pools tend to pay greater attention than larger colleges and universities to applicants' essays. Also, at some schools with large applicant pools, essays by applicants whose GPA and SAT scores fail to meet minimum or threshold requirements might go unread.

✎ WHO WILL READ AND EVALUATE MY ESSAY(S)?

Procedures vary among schools. Typically, however, one *admission officer* will read your essay(s) and write an evaluation. Admission officers are typically graduates, or *alumni*, of the school for which they work and are hired to evaluate applications; they do not, however, make final admission decisions. If you remain a viable candidate after the first "read," your essay(s) will then be scrutinized more closely by another admission officer or perhaps by the admission director or assistant director. Some schools (particularly small liberal arts colleges) will subject your essays to further scrutiny by circulating your file among members of an admission committee comprised of perhaps five to seven people (admission officials, faculty members, and possibly students).

✎ HOW DO SCHOOLS EVALUATE MY ESSAYS?

Evaluation methods vary somewhat among schools. Some schools, particularly larger institutions that process many applications, use a multiple-scoring system in which each essay receives separate scores for content, style, and mechanics. Other schools take a more holistic approach, relying on written comments by evaluators as well as dialogue among members of the admission committee.

LEARN MORE ABOUT YOURSELF

College admission personnel want to get to know you personally through your essays. How can they get to know who you really are if you

yourself are not really sure? Here are some self-discovery tools and techniques that will help ensure that the schools are meeting the *real* you through your essays.

✎ INTERVIEW YOUR FRIENDS AND RELATIVES

This can be a tough but very useful exercise. Try the following five questions; encourage your interview subjects to be brutally honest, and get ready to eat some humble pie:

1. How have you described me to people who haven't met me?

2. What's the best thing anyone has ever told you about me?

3. What's the worst thing anyone has ever told you about me?

4. What do you think is my most unusual or unique character trait?

5. What was your initial impression of me when you first met me? How has that changed?

✎ RECORD YOUR DREAMS

Nothing is more sincere and personal, and nothing is more unique and unusual, than a dream. You'll be amazed at the essay ideas you can dream up while you sleep!

✎ WRITE DOWN YOUR THOUGHTS AND FEELINGS ABOUT ISSUES THAT ARE MOST PERSONAL AND IMMEDIATE.

Let's face it: most 16- and 17-year olds are usually not as concerned with geopolitics and medieval literature as they are about more personal issues such as

- ✓ self-esteem (approval and validation of self, ideas, and values)
- ✓ identity
- ✓ independence from parents
- ✓ academic and extra-curricular success
- ✓ popularity and acceptance by a peer group
- ✓ sexuality, physical appearance, and attractiveness
- ✓ loyalty, trust, and honesty

Set aside some time every day to be alone and reflect on your own thoughts and feelings about these issues. If you keep a diary or journal, excerpts from these writings may very well provide the genesis of a highly effective essay.

✎ MAKE AN APPOINTMENT WITH YOUR HIGH SCHOOL COUNSELOR TO TALK ABOUT LIFE IN GENERAL.

Tell your counselor that you need assistance in learning more about yourself—who you really are and what you really want out of life. Be certain that you meet with a counselor you can trust to keep your conversation strictly confidential.

DO SOME SERIOUS BRAINSTORMING

Make the following exercises part of your daily routine for a month, and you'll be bursting at the seams with unique ideas for essays!

✎ RECORD OBSERVATIONS IN A "BELIEVE IT OR NOT" NOTEBOOK

Seemingly ordinary events can be quite interesting when viewed through a creative lens. Record interesting sights, bits of conversation, and events that you observe firsthand—at home, at school, and elsewhere. Try to see the unusual in the ordinary. Two masters of this art are George Carlin and Jerry Seinfeld, both of whom have a knack for finding something absurd about everyday happenings to which anyone can relate.

✎ BECOME A KEEN OBSERVER OF HUMAN BEHAVIOR.

Study the following behavior in people around you:

✓ introversion (shyness) and extroversion

✓ aggressiveness, assertiveness, and passivity

✓ friendliness and unfriendliness

✓ various kinds of intelligence, talent, and skill

✓ competitiveness and cooperation

✓ self-affirming behavior and self-defeating behavior

✎ READ THE EDITORIAL SECTION OF YOUR LOCAL NEWSPAPER

Newspaper editorial pages are chock-full of ideas for issue-related essays. These pages will also serve up good examples of effective as well as ineffective writing styles.

✎ SCAN THE MAGAZINE RACK AT THE LOCAL LIBRARY FOR PERIODICALS THAT LOOK INTERESTING TO YOU

Avoid the most popular titles, such as *Time* and *Newsweek*. Instead, take a look at periodicals such as *The New Yorker*.

✎ CHECK OUT COLLEGE-RELATED INTERNET RESOURCES

Web sites devoted to college admission are springing up like weeds these days. Check them out, and download everything you can about admission essays. Also, you might find discussions about college admission essays on various Internet bulletin boards.

✎ SURF THE WEB FOR INTERESTING ARTICLES AND ESSAYS.

Make note of potential topics and ideas for your essays, then use some of the Web's powerful search engines to find related Web sites. Also, don't forget to check out the many online magazines and periodicals, or *zines*, available on the Web.

✎ READ ESSAYS BY THE GREAT ESSAYISTS

Perhaps you're a bit insecure about your writing ability. Most great writers—as well as great artists and musicians—get to be great by emulating (but not mimicking) the masters. Take this as your cue. Go to the library and read essays by great essayists. After two hours in the library, you'll be oozing with inspiration—guaranteed. Use your favorite writer's style as a starting point for developing your own, as long as the style feels natural to you. Here's a list of writers to get you started:

> ✓ some contemporary essayists:
>> Calvin Trillin
>> Anna Quindlen
>> Dave Berry

✓ a few modern essayists:
> John Updike
> H.L. Mencken
> Tom Wolfe
> George Orwell

✓ some not-so-modern essayists:
> Henry Thoreau
> Ralph Waldo Emerson
> Jonathan Swift

✓ two writers who write about writing:
> William Zinsser
> E.B. White

✎ TAKE A FRESH LOOK AT ESSAYS THAT YOU HAVE ALREADY WRITTEN

Dust off those old essays you wrote for your English and creative writing classes. One of these essays may provide the genesis or inspiration for a great college admission essay. Resist the temptation, however, to take the easy way out by simply using one of these essays as your admission essay. Admission officers can smell recycled school papers a mile away!

CHECK OUT THE COLLEGE'S OWN RESOURCES FOR ESSAY IDEAS

Colleges themselves are great places to start gathering information and ideas for your essays. However, many applicants never think to look there. Here's a checklist for you to make sure you take advantage of all that a college has to offer you as an applicant.

✎ READ SEVERAL ISSUES OF THE SCHOOL NEWSPAPER

You'll learn what local and regional issues are important to the administration, faculty, and students. Certain newsworthy school events or happenings might strike you as particularly interesting, unique, shocking, or praiseworthy. Consider writing about such an issue or event in your essay for that school.

✎ READ THE ALUMNI PUBLICATIONS PRODUCED BY THE SCHOOL

Ask yourself: what values seem to be important to the administration and to the trustees? What image is the school attempting to convey? What are the school's policies and attitudes? What alumni accomplishments is the school touting? Perhaps these values, policies and accomplishments are worth addressing in your essay.

✎ TOUR THE CAMPUS WITH YOUR EYES WIDE OPEN

Observe the architecture, the sculptures, and other artwork around the campus. Read the plaques and engravings on, in, and around the buildings. Walk around the neighborhood surrounding the campus looking for essay nuggets in your path. If you can't visit the school in person, take an online tour of the school or obtain an information video from the school, if one is available. (Keep in mind, however, that schools' Web sites and videos are marketing tools as well as informational resources, so they may not present a completely objective picture of the school.)

✎ INVESTIGATE THE SCHOOL'S HISTORY

You'll be amazed at the inventive essay ideas that emerge. Here are just a few investigative questions to get you started:

✓ What were the political and economic circumstances surrounding the founding of the school? What were the founders' ideals and educational philosophies, and has the school moved away from its initial educational mission?

✓ Did the school ever serve as the subject, locale, or backdrop for an important historical event? What does that event mean to you?

✓ Who is the school's most famous alumni (or dropouts)? What are their accomplishments and impact upon you, the school, and society? Why did those individuals attend the college, and what kind of students were they?

✎ TALK TO CURRENT STUDENTS

Go to the central meeting place on campus, find some students who are hanging out (you won't have any trouble finding them), and strike up a

conversation. Ask them about life in the dormitory, fraternity, or sorority. Ask them what attracted them to the school initially and whether their initial perceptions about the school have changed. Ask them if they know any tales about legendary school pranks. You're sure to walk away with all sorts of essay ideas!

✎ READ WHAT THE ADMISSION APPLICATION SAYS ABOUT THE ESSAYS

A surprisingly large number of applicants ignore the directions and guidelines for essay writing that are spelled out in the school's application. Be sure you're not one of these students! Many schools include not only directions but also advice for writing the essay.

✎ CONTACT THE ADMISSION STAFF WITH UNANSWERED QUESTIONS ABOUT THE ESSAY

After you have read the application materials thoroughly, if any of the guidelines (concerning topic scope, page length, etc.) are still unclear, contact the school and ask for clarification. Don't be afraid to communicate with the school's admission staff yourself.

✎ VISIT THE SCHOOL'S WEB SITE

The Internet is probably the quickest and least expensive means of gathering information about colleges. Virtually all colleges and universities now make available online their school catalogues as well as admission policies, procedures, applications, and other information.

AVOID OVERUSED IDEAS: SEEK OUT OVERLOOKED IDEAS

Okay, you've just sat down with pen and paper (or mouse and monitor) to respond to a particular essay question. A brilliant, attention-grabbing, original idea immediately pops into your head. Before hastily committing your flash of genius to paper and rushing it to the admission committee, think again. Chances are that your initial original idea is anything but original. In this section we'll list some of the most overused ideas and suggest some alternative and fresh approaches.

✎ ESSAYS ABOUT PERSONAL RELATIONSHIPS AND INFLUENCES

In choosing a subject for an essay about a personal relationship or about someone you know personally who has influenced you, in addition to the more obvious choices, such as members of your immediate family or your best friend, consider subjects such as

✓ your favorite teacher

✓ your coach

✓ distant relatives (cousins, nieces, nephews) from other times or other places

✓ your arch-rival at school

✓ a student at school who is experiencing academic or social problems

✓ a neighbor

✓ penpals (or cyberfriends)

✓ a member of a friend's family

Don't write about your dog Spot or cat Fluffy. Admission officers have read far too many essays about family pets!

✎ ESSAYS ABOUT ISSUES

If asked to write about an issue of societal significance, keep in mind that that the following issues are discussed by many applicants:

✓ the environment

✓ world peace

✓ prejudice and discrimination

✓ drugs

✓ crime

If your personal experience or conviction strongly leads you to write on one of these topics, by all means go ahead. Otherwise, consider more neglected issues such as these:

✓ individual rights (e.g., right to die, AIDS, abortion, gun control, free speech)

✓ consumerism and materialism

✓ fairness, justice, and equity (but please don't mention O.J. Simpson)

✓ free trade among nations

✓ Internet issues (e.g., privacy, alienation, education, commerce)

✎ ESSAYS ABOUT YOUR EXPERIENCES OR ACTIVITIES OR ABOUT SIGNIFICANT EVENTS IN YOUR LIFE

Unless you have something highly intimate, unique, or creative to share with the reader about the experience, think again before you use any of the following as the focal point of your essay:

✗ the college admission process (especially the SAT and essay writing)

✗ your big trip to some faraway place, especially if you focus on:

how it enhanced your cultural awareness
how yucky the food was
how it taught you to accept people who were different
the *Wizard of Oz* angle (i.e., there's no place like home)

✗ wilderness and survival experiences; your exciting Outward Bound trek no doubt taught you to face your fears, to meet new challenges, and to rise to the occasion, but hundreds of other applicants have regaled admission officers with similar experiences

✗ winning or losing the big game, election, or other competition, if you use one of these tired themes:

it's not whether you win or lose
I now have greater self-confidence
I learned the importance of teamwork
I learned that my true talents lie elsewhere

✗ how all your discipline and hard work paid off in the end (the *Little Engine That Could* essay)

✗ summer camp

✗ a part-time job ("I learned more than I ever could have in school")

✗ your most unforgettable experience

Look elsewhere for personal experiences to share with the admission committee; for example:

✓ a seemingly ordinary school field trip or outing with friends or family that turned into an unexpected adventure or self-defining event

✓ a song, a poem, novel, or other serious literary or artistic work that made a genuine and deep impact on the way you look at yourself, others, the world around you, and life in general

✓ the time you received an unexpected gift from an unexpected source, or the time you spontaneously gave of yourself to someone or something

✓ a white lie, an off-the-cuff insulting remark, or a discourtesy (either yours or someone else's) that helped you to grow and mature in your understanding of yourself and others

✓ a contribution or accomplishment of yours motivated not by potential external reward but by some other force or reason

✓ an informal social situation that you replay over and over in your mind because it holds more meaning for you than seemingly more important events, such as holidays, weddings, or proms

✓ those times when teachers or other authority figures let their guard down for you, enabling you to approach them as an equal and as a friend

✎ ESSAYS ABOUT YOUR OWN PERSONAL QUALITIES

If the school's application calls for you to write about your own character, personality, likes, dislikes, or values, try to avoid these trite ideas and themes:

✗ lists of your favorite things or least-favorite things (please spare the admission officers your "sung to the tune of 'My Favorite Things' " masterpiece)

✗ your determination and tenacity; don't write about how you always get what you want or accomplish what you seek out to do

✗ how diverse you are in your interests and endeavors (the "Renaissance man" essay)

Instead, look inward at your quirky, seemingly less attractive, or downright negative traits. Don't be hesitant to expose a weakness or admit your fallibility. For example, don't be reluctant to talk about

✓ those little habits of yours that sometimes annoy those around you

✓ that time you really put your foot in your mouth

✓ a personal possession to which you have grown irrationally attached

✓ particular study habits that you would like to change

✓ your unusual awkwardness in certain social situations

OBSERVE THESE DOS AND DON'TS FOR THEME AND CONTENT

✓ **DO** write an essay that only you could honestly write. If it's possible that the reader will read anything similar from any other applicant, go back to the drawing board.

✓ **DO** convey a positive message overall. Cynicism will not score points with the admission committee.

✓ **DO** strive for depth, not breadth. Focus on one event or idea rather than trying to cover an entire subject. Think personal and anecdotal.

✓ **DO** reject your first idea or angle. It's probably been used a million times.

✓ **DO** be interesting but more important, be yourself. Convey your true and genuine thoughts and feelings; don't try to portray yourself as someone with interests, values, and opinions that aren't really yours.

✓ **DO** write about what you know and have observed or experienced firsthand, *not* about things that are beyond your personal development as a teenager. Book knowledge or other secondhand information does not convey to the reader any sense of who you are.

✓ **DO** write about something you feel strongly about. If you write on a topic about which you have little interest or knowledge, your lack of sincerity and enthusiasm will show.

✓ **DO** write about other people as well as about yourself. We are defined as individuals largely in terms of our experiences with others, and acknowledging this through your essay will help ensure that you don't appear overly self-centered.

✓ **DO** be experiential, but avoid too much imagery. Relate to the reader the full scope of an experience—sights, sounds, and perhaps even smells. Be careful, however, not to overuse imagery; otherwise, the result may be a forced, unnatural style that gives the reader the impression that you are trying too hard to be creative.

✗ **DON'T** let others—especially your parents—decide for you what to write. Feel free to brainstorm with others for ideas, but don't ask: "What should I write about?"

✗ **DON'T** try to sell yourself or prove anything by convincing the reader how great you are, how smart you are, or how accomplished you are. Your definitive theories and brilliant solutions to global problems will not impress the reader. Admit it: you have many more questions than answers at this point in your life. Use your essay as an opportunity to wonder about life, to pose thoughtful questions, and to probe and investigate, *not* to tell the reader "the way it is."

✗ **DON'T** try to write an important or scholarly essay. A well-researched essay that shows off your knowledge of a particular academic subject tells the reader nothing about you. The reader will only suspect that your essay is actually a recycled term paper.

✗ **DON'T** try to guess what the admission committee wants you to write. This approach will result in a "safe" essay that will fall flat.

✗ **DON'T** rehash what the reader already knows about you. Don't reiterate accomplishments or activities that are already mentioned elsewhere in your application.

✗ **DON'T** appear overly idealistic. World peace and a clean environment are worthy ideals, but avoid coming across as preachy or fanatic. There are always at least two sides to every controversial issue, so recognize the merits of all sides. Otherwise, you might sound a bit naive.

✗ **DON'T** waste your essay opportunity to explain blemishes or deficiencies in your application. A low grade, a low SAT score, or an absence of extracurricular activities is not a worthy subject for discussion in your essay. If you must defend a blemish in your record, contact the school and ask (anonymously) if you can attach a separate (and brief) explanation as an addendum to your application. As an alternative, ask your college counselor to clarify these points in his or her recommendation letter.

✗ **DON'T** write anything that might embarrass the reader or make him or her feel uncomfortable. There's nothing wrong with discussing sensitive topics such as substance abuse, sexuality, spirituality, religious beliefs, and political views. Just be sure to treat the subject gingerly, avoid generalizations, and use a respectful tone. Otherwise, you may put off or even offend the reader.

✗ **DON'T** write an essay that reads like a newspaper editorial. The schools welcome your opinions, but don't get on a soap box and appear overly critical of other viewpoints.

✗ **DON'T** even think about mentioning popular television shows, movies, musicians, or actors, regardless of how significant they are to you; and please don't mention any Dr. Suess book. (The wastebaskets in admission offices fill to the brim every fall with Dr. Suess essays.)

WRITE, WRITE, AND WRITE SOME MORE

Anyone who has ever sat down to write an open-ended essay has experienced some degree of writer's block or paralysis. Sometimes the biggest problem is just getting the words flowing. Here are some useful tips that will help get your pencil (or keyboard keys) moving.

✎ TRY SOME STREAM-OF-CONSCIOUSNESS SPEED DRILLS

Pick a topic (any topic), then fill up a piece of paper with words as fast as you possibly can in a stream-of-consciousness fashion. You may find it helpful to impose a time limit on yourself. Don't worry about content, style, or grammar; just loosen up that pencil!

✎ KEEP ALL YOUR DRAFTS, EVEN YOUR ROUGHEST ONES

As you write first drafts, don't worry about grammar. Keep all your drafts, even the roughest ones. Writing is like any other creative endeavor—for some people the initial effort produces the best result, while for others a superior product results from a long process of crafting and fine-tuning.

✎ START WITH THE FOUR COMMON APPLICATION QUESTIONS

Carry around a notepad and jot down your thoughts on these topics as you think of them, without trying to organize them. Stimulate your thinking even more by bouncing your thoughts off others during your everyday conversations; as soon as possible, jot down the ideas that emerged during those conversations. You might discover your best essay right there on your notepad.

✎ EXPRESS YOUR IDEAS AND OPINIONS FREELY ON THE INTERNET

Post your writing anonymously to appropriate issue-related newsgroups and bulletin boards. This might help you overcome writer's block, and you might obtain some useful feedback that will stimulate more ideas and help you to fine-tune your essays. However, don't give away your ideas or essays by posting them on college admission bulletin boards.

✎ KNOW WHEN YOU ARE FINISHED

Don't write forever! At some point, leave well enough alone, print out your essay, and submit it. Bear in mind that beyond a certain point, additional editing, fine-tuning, and revising will probably result in an essay that is well-written but lacking in character and distinctiveness— not the end result that you want!

IMPRESS THEM WITH YOUR STYLE... BUT DON'T RESORT TO GIMMICKS

Your writing style—format, structure, syntax, tone, word choice, and the like—may play just as important a role as content in the school's overall evaluation of your essay. Strive to develop a style that is natural, somewhat informal, and distinctly your own. Here are some more specific guidelines.

✎ STRUCTURE AND FORMAT OF THE ESSAY

Each school will, of course, impose its own guidelines and restrictions as to essay length. Otherwise, the format and structure is left largely to the writer. Here are five important points to keep in mind:

1. Short essays are generally preferable to long ones. An essay that is concise and to the point will be appreciated by the reader. Do not take this advice too far, however. Be careful not to sacrifice substance or cut your message short merely for brevity's sake. (You will notice some effective longer essays in Part 2 of this book.) Also, one-word and one-sentence essays have been tried a thousand times but have not worked once.

2. Use logical, frequent paragraph breaks at points where you think the reader could use a break. Don't limit yourself to the five-paragraph essay format you learned in English class.

3. Avoid poetry unless it's the only way to get your message across and you are quite good at it. Sonnets, limericks, haiku, and "sung to the tune of . . ." essays have been tried many times, so think again before abandoning good-old prose.

4. Drawings, cartoons, and other visual devices are best left to serious artists. If drawing or graphic arts is your passion and potential career, by all means present yourself through this medium to the college's art department (especially if you're really good). Otherwise, don't.

5. So you want to be a lawyer someday? Please don't write an essay in the form of a contract or court document. Is it your dream to become a physician? Don't write your essay in the form of prescription. Got the general idea?

✎ FINDING AN APPROPRIATE AND GENUINE STYLE AND TONE

In an attempt to get noticed, don't resort to an extreme or gimmicky writing style that doesn't reflect your true "voice." The appropriate tone and style should emerge naturally from the message you wish to convey. Here are five specific points of advice to bear in mind:

1. Strive to write in a style that reads like a telephone conversation with a friend, without all the "uhm"s, "like"s, and "you know"s.

2. Don't try too hard to be funny. It's okay to be lighthearted and to show a dry and subtle humor about your topic, but don't write a humorous essay *per se*. No puns, please!

3. Be forceful and opinionated, but don't insult or offend. A bit of irreverence in your tone and attitude is perfectly accept-able—in fact, the reader will find it refreshing. However, an overly flippant or disrespectful tone might suggest that you don't take the essay or the admission process very seriously.

4. Avoid whining, complaining, or appearing bitter, sarcastic, angry, caustic, boastful, or aggressive.

5. Avoid coming across as overly humble.

✎ THE ALL-IMPORTANT OPENING SENTENCES

First impressions are important. Strive to engage the reader immediately with an opener that will make him or her want to read on. Avoid trite and hackneyed introductions—specifically:

✗ Don't introduce yourself to the admission committee—for example, "Hello, my name is . . ."

✗ Don't ask the reader's permission to tell him or her about yourself—for example, "Please permit me to discuss my . . ."

✗ Stay away from term-paper style introductory paragraphs. Don't reiterate the topic or question or itemize the points you will make in subsequent paragraphs. In other words, break all the rules you learned in class for writing term papers.

Okay, then how *should* you begin your essay? Try taking your cue from comedians who know how to capture an audience's interest right from the start. Tune in to some stand-up comedy shows on television and take notes. Here are some opening angles to consider:

✓ an enigmatic statement that makes the reader wonder to what or to whom you are referring

✓ an obscure quotation (avoid popular quotations or quotations from famous people)

✓ a thoughtful question

✓ a trivial observation that anyone can relate to but that nobody else would ever think to mention in an essay

✓ a paradox

✓ a gross generalization

✓ someone else's opinion or theory

✓ a confession

✓ an overly obvious statement

✎ ESSAY ENDINGS

Notice that we use the term "ending" here instead of "conclusion" or "summary." This is because conclusions and summaries are for term papers, not for your admission essay. Here are a few DOs and DON'Ts to ensure that your essay ends with a bang, not a bomb:

✓ **DO** provide closure—a sense that you have provided the reader with bookends to your essay or that you have come full circle by the end of your essay.

✓ **DO** use the final sentences to end any suspense and to answer any question that you might have posed earlier in the essay.

✓ **DO** use short, forceful sentences to end your essay.

✗ **DON'T** address the admission committee or ask them to admit you.

✗ **DON'T** use words like "finally," "in sum," or "in conclusion."

✗ **DON'T** repeat or sum up in any way.

✗ **DON'T** end your essay with a quotation.

✎ INCLUDING A TITLE FOR YOUR ESSAY

Is it a good idea to precede your essay with a brief, attention-grabbing title? The use of titles is acceptable but superfluous in the eyes of the reader, who is far more concerned with the content of the essay itself. Go ahead and use a title if you think it would help communicate your message or if you have a great idea for a title that you can't resist using; otherwise, don't. By the way, some of the essays in Part 2 of this book originally included titles, although most did not. (The essay titles are not included in Part 2.)

✎ WORD CHOICE

Words are the building blocks for communicating ideas. Without a strong foundation, your message will be ineffective. While word choice depends on your personal writing style and your message, there are certain kinds of words you should avoid in your essay.

✗ **AVOID** words that are used over and over on resumes, in job descriptions, and in books of virtues. These words are guaranteed to result in a dry, dull style and a potentially boastful tone. Here are just a few examples:

responsibility	goal
interact	role
develop	integrity
leadership	excellence
interpersonal	

✗ **AVOID** slang and currently popular buzz phrases. You'll be "dissed" and "brutalized" by the admission committee, so write your essay in this style—NOT!

✗ **AVOID** superfluous words and phrases, including "courtroom" rhetoric, waffle words, needless self-references, and transition words. Here are a few examples:

rhetoric:
   clearly
   obviously
   unquestionably

waffle words:
   somewhat
   rather
   quite
   perhaps

self-references:
   I think
   I believe
   my feeling is that

transition words:
   first, second, third, finally
   thus, in conclusion
   moreover
   however
   the next point

✗ **AVOID** technical, scientific, and obscure "SAT-style" words. A plethora of garish periphrasis may come across as haughty or supercilious. Get the idea?

✎ STYLISTIC DEVICES—DOS AND DON'TS

All great writers have their favorite literary devices that distinguish their writing. Here are some devices to help make your essay shine, along with some others to avoid:

✓ **DO** use analogies (metaphors and similes) to help convey your message, but don't overdo it.

✓ **DO** incorporate dialogue into your essay, but think twice about using a screenplay approach (unless you plan to major in the theater arts).

✓ **DO** use more short sentences than long ones. Don't take this to an extreme, however. Mix up sentence length so that your essay flows naturally and rhythmically when read aloud.

✓ **DO** use logical paragraph breaks to provide a visual break for the reader and to indicate a change in direction, train of thought, or idea. Don't set off any one sentence as a separate paragraph, except for dialogue or for dramatic impact.

✓ **DO** use the active voice instead of the passive voice. In most cases, the active voice is preferred. Here's an example of each:

> *(active)* The applicant wrote an outstanding essay.

> *(passive)* A less-than-outstanding essay was written by the applicant.

✗ **DON'T** tell the reader explicitly, in effect: "I am a unique and interesting person." Instead, let the reader glean this from your interesting and unique essay.

✗ **DON'T** mimic or parody a well-known writer or literary work. If the writer or work is unfamiliar to the reader, your essay might look pretty silly! Worse yet, if the reader knows and admires the author's work, you might offend the reader.

✗ **DON'T** be a dummy by dabbling in dumb alliterations.

✗ **DON'T** start too many sentences with the word "I."

✗ **DON'T** use the phrase "a lot of." A lot of applicants use "a lot of" a lot of times. There are a lot of other choices—such as "many," "numerous," and "significant."

✗ **DON'T** necessarily write entirely in complete sentences. A complete sentence includes both a subject and a predicate. Remember? The previous sentence wasn't really a sentence, was it? Nevertheless, it could be quite acceptable in an essay if it flows naturally and is useful for emphasis or stylistic impact.

AVOID CARELESS ERRORS AND GRAMMATICAL BLUNDERS

The schools will not penalize you for one or two minor mechanical or grammatical errors. Glaring or frequent errors may, however, adversely affect your chances of admission. Above all, make sure that you heed the following two pieces of advice:

1. There's no excuse for spelling errors in your essay! Don't just run your essay through a spell-checking program. Spell-checkers don't catch words that may be spelled correctly in some other context but not as they are used in your essay. Four example, the first word in this sentence would slip past a spell-checker, wouldn't it?!

2. You'd better get the name of the school right! Otherwise, you'll insult the reader and appear careless and sloppy. Is the school a "College" or "University"? Is it "University of . . ." or ". . . University"? Have you inadvertently used the name of another school to which you are sending a similar essay?

As for grammar, there are literally thousands of grammatical blunders that you might potentially commit in writing your essay. It would be futile to attempt to cover the rules of grammar here. The best way to ensure that your essay is grammatically correct is to refer to a comprehensive grammar guide. Here are three good ones:

1. *Prentice Hall Reference Guide to Grammar and Usage*, by Muriel Harris, published by Prentice Hall.

2. *Harbrace College Handbook*, by John C. Hodges, et al., 12th Edition, Published by Harcourt Brace Johanovich, College & School Division.

3. *MLA Handbook for Writers of Research Papers*, by Joseph Gibaldi, 4th Edition, published by the Modern Language Association of America.

Also, don't forget about another invaluable resource: your high school English teacher.

OBTAIN USEFUL FEEDBACK AND FINE-TUNE YOUR ESSAY

Here are 10 tips and techniques to help you obtain useful feedback that will result in the most effective possible essay:

1. When showing your essay to others, avoid asking, "Do you like it?" Instead, ask something like: "If you didn't know me, what would you say about the person who wrote this essay?"

2. Set aside each draft for several days, then go back to it. It's quite possible that a particular point or idea that you thought was so brilliant or clever one day will come across as corny or downright inane a week later.

3. Post bits and pieces of rough drafts to topically relevant Internet newsgroups and bulletin boards, then check back for reactions. Don't let on, however, that your posted articles pertain to your college admission essays.

4. Try to imagine that you're flipping television channels, and on one channel someone is reading your essay aloud. Would you change channels, or would you be intrigued enough to stay tuned to that channel to hear the rest of the story?

5. People who you ask for feedback probably have not worked in the admission field, so take their advice with a grain of salt!

6. Join or start an essay writing club at your high school. Feedback from classmates can be just as valuable as feedback from teachers and other adults.

7. Don't ask too many people to read your essay. Your own voice might get lost as a result of your critics' comments and suggestions.

8. Although it may be painful, don't be reluctant to discard an essay and start from scratch. If you've revised it again and again but are still not pleased with it, you're probably on the wrong track and need a fresh, new approach.

9. Converse with others about the topic of your essay, without letting on that you are relating its substance. You'll get far more candid responses with this approach.

10. If others describe your essay as cute, humorous, or clever, go back to your word processor and try to be less cute, humorous, or clever. After reading your essay, do others describe you as: mature, responsible, organized, hard-working, accomplished, determined, principled, or nice? If so, you're probably on the wrong track. Here are some key feedback words and phrases that indicate you are on the *right* track with your essay: delightful, wonderful, affectionate, warm, lighthearted, savvy, elegant, insightful, sensitive, fun, thoughtful, genuine, vivid, wow, I'd like to meet . . . , I can really relate. . . .

PACKAGE AND PRESENT YOUR ESSAY APPROPRIATELY

If you are submitting a paper-based application, don't underestimate the importance of your essay's physical appearance. Make sure that it is easy to read and that it makes a positive visual impression. Here are some specific points to keep in mind.

✎ IF THE SCHOOL PERMITS IT, PRESENT YOUR ESSAY ON A SEPARATE SHEET OF PAPER

However, resist any temptation to catch the reader's attention by using odd-sized paper, colored paper, letterhead, personalized stationery, or paper with preprinted pictures (e.g., smile faces) or phrases (e.g., "From the desk of . . ."). Use plain, white, high-quality, 8½" × 11" paper only, please.

✎ NUMBER EACH PAGE OF YOUR ESSAY, AND INCLUDE YOUR NAME AND SOCIAL SECURITY NUMBER ON EACH PAGE

This will ensure that your essays aren't lost or jumbled and will demonstrate your attention to detail.

✎ ASSEMBLE YOUR ESSAYS PROPERLY

Most schools indicate a particular order for you to assemble and present the various essays as well as other parts of your application. Be sure to comply with these guidelines or instructions. Use staples only if the school requests it.

✎ BE SURE TO COMPLY STRICTLY WITH ANY PAGE LIMITS THAT THE SCHOOL IMPOSES

Don't use small margins, line spacing, or fonts to squeeze a long essay onto a prescribed number of pages. Go back and shorten your essay instead. (Remember, brevity is a virtue in the eyes of admission officials.)

✎ DON'T WORRY TOO MUCH ABOUT THE SCHOOL'S WORD LIMITS

Nobody is going to count words or penalize you if you've exceeded the limit by a small margin. Try not to exceed the limit by more than ten percent, however. (This applies to electronic applications as well.)

✎ DON'T WRITE YOUR ESSAY IN LONGHAND

A handwritten essay would be justifiable, however, if either (1) the school requests it, (2) calligraphy is a serious hobby of yours, or (3) the subject of your essay in some way involves handwriting.

✎ USE HIGHLY READABLE FONTS

Fonts with serifs (stems at the tops and bottoms of the letters) are generally more readable than sans-serif fonts (fonts without the stems). Choose a readable point size (11–12 point). Don't use a gimmicky or fancy typeface. Finally, not all font software is comparable in quality. In a poor quality typeface, the "kerning" (spaces between letters) may be uneven, creating a sloppy visual impression.

✎ INCLUDE AMPLE MARGINS

Use 1″–1¼″ margins on all sides, unless the school specifies otherwise. That way your essay looks more appealing, and readers have space to write comments. Don't format your essay in columns.

✎ PRINT YOUR FINAL ESSAY ON A HIGH-RESOLUTION LASER PRINTER

Ink-jet print might smear or smudge. Use at least a 600 × 600 dpi (dots per inch) printer, if possible, for crisp, clean characters. Avoid colors—black text on white paper is best.

✎ DO NOT SUBMIT ESSAYS ON VIDEOTAPE OR AUDIOTAPE

If you have a terrific message but feel that you can convey that message effectively only through a medium other than print, check with the school first to see if they will allow it. Please don't refer the reader to your World Wide Web home page. It's *not* a novel idea, and admission personnel simply do not have the time for this.

✎ THINK TWICE BEFORE INCLUDING SUPPLEMENTARY MATERIALS

Unless the school encourages you to do so, do *not* submit to the admission office supplementary materials such as samples of your artwork, musical recordings or compositions, other writing samples, your science project, and the like. If you feel strongly that these materials would help your chances of admission, contact the school and ask whether you can send samples of your work to the appropriate academic department.

PART 2

50 Great Essays

Okay, you now know a lot more about how to write an effective college admission essay. It would sure help, though, to see some essays that illustrate the advice in Part 1, wouldn't it? Look no further—they're right here!

All of the sample essays in Part 2 are authentic—written and submitted by successful applicants to real colleges. The essays here are quite diverse because the questions to which they respond are different and because each student brings his or her own style, personality, and "voice" to the essay. (Keep in mind as you read these samples, however, that some references to specific persons, schools, and other entities have been deleted.)

Don't even think about copying the sample essays in this book. They are intended to illustrate the advice and suggestions offered by admission officials as well as to inspire you and to spark ideas of your own; but they are *not* for copying. By plagiarizing a sample essay in this book, you will not only violate federal copyright laws but will also jeopardize your chances for admission to the college of your choice, since admission officials at many colleges will have read this book and will be on the lookout for essays that resemble the ones here.

A REVEALING LOOK AT THE REAL ME *(7 Essays)*

Essay No. 1

I can't tell you in which peer group I'd fit best because I'm a social chameleon and am comfortable in most; I will instead describe my own social situation and the various cliques I drift in and out of.

My high school's student body is from a part of town that is much more diverse than the rest of the city, and the city as a whole is more diverse than most of the state. The location of my school, only a few blocks from the University of Oregon, is greatly responsible for the social atmosphere. Whereas the other high schools in town draw mainly from middle-class white suburban families, mine sits in the division between the poor west university neighborhood and the affluent east university one. East university is hilly and forested with quiet residential streets and peaceful, large houses. A few blocks west, using the university as the divider, the houses become small and seedy. On the west side of my school there are many dirty apartments; crime is high and social status is low.

The result is the presence of two very distinct social scenes in the school itself. What is ironic although not crucial to this essay is that the school, a squat, gray-stained concrete sprawl, is divided right through the middle, just as its surrounding neighborhood is. The west wing ends in a gym, a symbol of lower-class recreation, and low aspiration, while the east wing holds the auditorium, the stronghold of sophistication, highbrow musical and theatrical achievement. On the east side are artsy wall murals, on the west side only graffiti.

The west parking lot holds mostly dirty pickup trucks, low-rider gangster cars and dilapidated, inherited little Hondas. The east lot is the home of numerous Mercedes and Chevy Suburbans, the gas-guzzlers and the late-models. The A.P. classes are strongly rooted in the east end; the remedial ones are clustered around the west athletic facilities. I burden you with this description in order to display the split, both social and geographic, that characterizes my academic life.

My classes are almost entirely on the east end of school; I'm attracted to them in a polar fashion as if I were a positively charged little

scholastic particle, happily magnetized to the center of learning. However, despite the fact that I am fully integrated and comfortable in the intellectual east-end society, the stereotypical education robot is something I am not. My primary social scene is a contrast to the nerd-set.

Understand that I'm a snowboarder and that the Oregon snowboard culture is not some obscure athletic fringe group; on the contrary, it is quite defined, almost established in the mainstream. It is complete with its own dialect, style and customs. The rest of the snowboarders in school are undeniably members of the west halls and their houses are on the wrong side of the university.

I spend my lunches with my fellow nerds. We go to coffee shops and delis. I'm accepted as one of them. My larger-than-normal pants and similar statements of snow-style are recognized as superficial. However, I spend my weekends with the other crew. We go to parties and up to the mountain. We share the same discoloration of our faces, tan and leathery on the cheeks and forehead, pale around the eyes. Our faces bear the scars of wearing snowboarding goggles too often in the bright sun, and are proof of our membership in the snow posse, as indelible as the ornate tattoos that show gang alliances. Our tans demand respect from the kids in the west halls, for they are our social credentials in that end of the school, equivalent to standing on the varsity football team. Once associated with grungy skateboarders, the snowboard culture has found its own niche, just as surfing did before it. We now show much more similarity to jocks than to skater punks.

When I'm with my classmates, I'm one of them—a cultivated, upper-class young man. I'm invited to their houses and speak to their parents on a polite first name basis. When I hang out with boarders and jocks, I'm invited to their refuges and speak the rapidly shifting socialect. Very few of the students in my school drift socially as I do. As a result of the recent American infatuation with the alternative sub-culture, my classmates give me respect for embodying an unconventional trend while preserving my proper social standing. In the same sense, my clan from the wrong end of the school respects me for remaining faithful to our culture while succeeding academically; in their eyes I have found a way to get out of the social hole without selling out.

I'm perfectly comfortable with the fact that I don't have one single social identity. I think that if I only felt comfortable among kids from a certain end of the school, my life would be less interesting.

✎   ✎   ✎

Essay No. 2

Last year, when the Duke football team beat Virginia and students carried the north goal-post to the main quad, I was one of many who scratched their names into the uprights. But there was one difference: I scratched "Stephen Byers, Class of 2000." For that one instant, I belonged to Duke, and Duke belonged to me.

Two-and-a-half years ago, I visited Duke for the first time with my older sister. I was the first to say, "This is where I want to go to college." Jenn was angry with her little brother for that remark because the trip was meant for her. That brief visit, and all others that followed, increased my determination to be accepted one day as a student at Duke. Having visited the campus many times over the past year, I have witnessed firsthand the academic challenge of the classroom experience as well as getting a taste of the university's social side. Since my first visit, I have met many Duke students who are genuinely excited about expanding their knowledge and about the challenging education that Duke provides.

Along with what Duke can offer me, I believe I have much to contribute to Duke. At the end of Easter mass in Page Auditorium last year, I discovered what community service means to students at Duke. As a graduating senior walked across the stage, she appeared composed and confident. After reaching the podium, she slowly described her role as a "big sister" to a young girl in Durham. Her voice began to crack. Composed again, she pleaded for someone to take over her responsibility to this girl. Even though the student was graduating within a month, she refused to leave Duke until someone agreed to take over her role. She was a young woman who really cared.

I have similar feelings for a brain-damaged girl with whom I work as a therapy volunteer. Petra has given me more than I could ever give her in return, and I will not stop giving what I can to others when I leave for college. I hope to encourage fellow classmates to get involved with

service work in the Duke community because I know how rewarding volunteer work can be.

When I first realized I wanted to go to Duke, it was because my sister was looking at a top university. It was then that my dream to attend Duke began—a dream that I hope will soon become a reality.

✎ ✎ ✎

Essay No. 3

There is something you should know about me right off the bat. It's not something I confess lightly, but here goes: I am an optimist. There, now that I've said it, I feel better. It's not as though I haven't tried to give it up; I have. But I keep going back to it like a duck to water. What's so bad about being an optimist?

I was born with a joyful nature. I reportedly smiled the entire time I was in the nursery, and for the next four years or so I slept twenty out of twenty-four hours every day. Life already was a dream come true for me, but when I finally regained consciousness I experienced what turned out to be my earliest memory. It was a conversation with my father about my confusion as to whether a glass was half-empty of half-full. My father, at first, figured it was the "half" concept which baffled me, but it turned out to be the "empty" part I didn't get. He officially declared me an optimist on the spot, and the label stuck.

The news got around fast. The kids in the neighborhood discovered my flaw when I played peewee soccer. Our team, the Green Slime, almost always lost, which tended to dilute the enthusiasm of the players. Except for me, that is. Even with the score 14 to 0 in the last minute of the last quarter, I would be running up and down the field yelling "Score, score, score!" resulting in my teammates' kicking the ball *at* me rather than to me. My grandmother discovered my optimism while we were watching a movie on television. In one scene, a car skidded through a guard rail, bounced off the side of a cliff, exploded into a ball of fire and plunged into the sea a hundred feet below. I turned to my grandmother and cheerfully said, "That wouldn't necessarily kill you, you know," prompting her to exchange meaningful glances with my mother, apparently questioning my judgment or sanity, or both.

Soon I was going to school where my former teammates had to put up with me as a classmate. My habit of waving my hand to answer any question and talking cheerfully about nearly every subject, no matter how catastrophic, did not endear me to them. My optimism even got to my teacher. She became fed up with my dismissal of her favorite topics—pollution, global warming and endangered species—as nothing to worry about. Unable to attack me directly, perhaps due to my good spelling and reading quiz scores, she took out her anger on my poor messy desk. In order to embarrass me, she made me empty everything out of my "cubby" and desk onto the floor and stand in front of the class. For the first time in my life, I was aware that perhaps not everyone thought well of me, and I became concerned and confused. After that, I kept my desk neat and clean, but my spirit was dampened. Had this sort of experience continued, I suppose I might have turned out like everyone else. But as luck would have it, my mother decided at this point to pull my sister and me out of class for home schooling.

In home schooling I was allowed the freedom to explore the world as I wished. I didn't have to read about whatever catastrophe people were currently bemoaning, and so I feasted on the Italian Renaissance, the novels of Victor Hugo, and the movies by Frank Capra, Billy Wilder, and Ernst Lubitsch. During these years of degenerate self-indulgence, my optimism flowered like algae in an aquarium.

I eventually dropped back into school because I decided that I should get a diploma since I wanted to go to college, and for a time my father actually held out hope that my optimism might be cured. The return to school, however, had little effect, for by that time I was a recognized and confirmed optimist with little hope of recovery.

Perhaps with time I will one day become cynical and mature, losing my naive, childish beliefs. But for the time being, I'll make a confession: I don't think I will. The truth is, I intend to keep on being an optimist. After all, here we are clinging to a tiny speck of dust called Earth, hurtling through space and going who knows where. And all we have is this little time squeezed between two great silences. So what is there to be pessimistic about?

✎   ✎   ✎

Essay No. 4

When I was four years old I decided to challenge conventional notions of the human limit by flying through a glass window. The impetus was Superman, whose exploits on television had induced my experiment. Nine stitches and thirteen years later, while I no longer attempt to be stronger than steel or faster than a speeding bullet, I still find myself testing my limits, mental and physical.

It seems that I have spent my life getting into one thing or another. From that ill-fated flight to my recent trials and tribulations trying to repair my personal computer, I try to involve myself in as many things as I can. You could call me curious. Some people are apprehensive about being labeled "curious," associating the word with mischief and prying, but I think the word fits who I am. After all, "curious" is defined as "eager to acquire knowledge."

I'm eager. When I was in kindergarten my teacher told my father I was a hyperactive and unruly child. Claiming no kid of his was "hyperactive," my father promptly took me out of the school. To be honest, Dad wasn't completely right. I am a person who can never sit still. My sister calls me a time bomb when I drive because my hands are always fidgeting with the radio dials, the air conditioner, and other gadgets. When I want something, I can't wait. As an anxious eight year old, I remember driving my family nuts in anticipation of that staple of the 80's family, the Nintendo. I remember spending the night before pitching for my baseball team in the district playoffs polishing my cleats and organizing everything so it would be perfect. Now I spend sleepless nights dreaming about my future—what I'm going to do, where I'm going to be, and how I'm going to get there.

I am eager to acquire knowledge. For my ninth birthday, my father gave me a set of the *World Book Encyclopedia*. Although I would rather have received a set of transformers, as I look back I realize that my Dad made the right decision. While I have not read every volume of the encyclopedia from cover to cover, it is safe to say that when opened, the books don't close right back up again. As a kid I made it a practice to read a few pages every day before I went to sleep. The way I look at it, all that trivia is prepping me for Jeopardy!

You can call me curious. You can call me eager to acquire knowledge. You can call me Isaac.

✎   ✎   ✎

Essay No. 5

Thinking. Plato did it, Freud studied it, Rodin sculpted it. Learning to do it critically can be difficult. Some never learn how, while for others it just comes naturally. I personally have "thought" the vast majority of my life. It was a talent I never considered. I just practiced. A friend once bought me a button that read, "I think, therefore I'm dangerous." He said it described me well. I suppose he was right.

I cultivated my thinking in seventh grade. I was in a gifted and talented program deep in Mandeville, Louisiana. We studied from books dug out of high-school dumpsters. Class was held in an old garage with makeshift classrooms that carried throughout the building the voice of each conjecture, the fire across each synapse. Some sixty of us studied there, bombarded by that barrage of thought. There was a real energy in that secondhand atmosphere, though. Our teachers did more than promote lofty erudite conversation; that makeshift environment encouraged real-life application of our lessons. We learned to read like thinkers, write like thinkers, experiment like thinkers. We evolved into real students.

Until I went to Mandeville, I considered my "giftedness" something rather unremarkable, even burdensome. All it seemed to bring me was extra homework in my Gifted-and-Talented class, boredom in the regular classroom, and estrangement from my peers. Junior high changed all of that. During my middle-school years I didn't learn about peer pressure, high hair or kissing. I learned how to balance chemical equations. I learned how to write eight-page term papers. I learned "mastication," "genre," and "tatterdemalion." Being an anomaly of the pre-teen world was legitimate there. I was gifted, and I was fine.

Mandeville's G/T program was truly extraordinary. Twenty-eight of us, from all walks of life, banded together there in a rather strange group. We didn't all get along, but a sense of respect infused our relationships and our classrooms. We were all spared labels like "nerd"

and "brain." We bonded through a tremendous connection: the capabilities of our minds. A sense of family developed based on our similar learning experience. Having challenging material presented to us was an enthralling treat. I was so eager to consume and digest this newfound knowledge that I never stopped to doubt myself. I was too busy learning to doubt. I developed real confidence in my strengths as a student.

The support system we developed in those years made a substantial difference in how we handled our giftedness. When I started school at age four, my teachers hailed me as a genius, a prodigy with a photographic memory. Halfway through first grade, I was advanced another year. All the grand prognostications and expectations came crashing down. I did not have the memory. I could not handle the transfer. I was not a prodigy. I always felt I had disappointed these people in some way; I never wanted to let them down. My experience at Mandeville helped me to accept my disability as well as my ability. None of us were geniuses, but we all knew that we were still talented individuals. Intelligent, not brilliant. And that was okay.

I had to leave that school after two years. My mom decided it was time for her to return to school, a goal that could be obtained by moving back to the Great White North. We moved to Cloquet, Minnesota in 1988. Despite boasting the only Frank Lloyd Wright designed service station, Cloquet was no home to the higher world of academia. It was the home of a paper mill. I returned to a school world some might call reality; I was a "brain" and a "geek" again. Lucky for me that I had already learned the value of my mind. Although I've done more than my share of self-doubting, I know that I am a thinker. I know what I love to learn, and that in this, I am not alone.

✎   ✎   ✎

Essay No. 6

The sky was mottled with clumps of white. I stood on the border between the track and the field, my eyes intently fixed on one particular clump. As the wind rustled by, the white began to fade from view. I remained fixated. The cloud became wisps, and the wisps, in turn, became smaller and bluer until there was no white remaining. I blinked and turned away.

My Theory of Knowledge teacher, Mr. Coleman, defines cloud-poofing as the willful dissipation of a small cloud. The process is simple: one selects the cloud for extinction, concentrates on the chosen cloud, and wills it to dissipate. Intending to master the art of cloud poofing, my class marched outside on a windy April afternoon. Along with the others, I planted myself in one spot and stared up at the sky. After everyone had poofed at least one cloud, we reentered the building, and, as part of our discussion, divided into two factions: the believers and the non-believers. Everyone, that is, except for me.

The skeptic, a logician, would say that the weather that day was no accident, that had we ventured outside on a windless day, the experiment would have failed. He would attribute the clouds' sudden disappearance to gusts of wind. All clouds, he would continue, form and then dissipate. We were an irrelevance. The "creatician," in contrast, would claim that the skeptic has been influenced by societal conventions. Less affected by science and logic, the creatician would see no reason why the mind could not affect the clouds, and know that the skeptic cannot, no matter how hard he tries, prove otherwise.

I am the logician. I am the creatician. In that classroom, surrounded by the noise of fervent discussion, I felt the resurgence of a conflict I had come to know well. The two sides of my personality had begun to vie for intellectual supremacy. Part of my mind, the logical side, agreed with the logician in saying that not only is the simplest explanation the best one but also that the mind has no power to alter external stimuli.

"Logic," preaches the logician. "Remember and heed logic."

"Wait!" retorts the science disregarder, the creatician. "You, logician, have no proof that the mind is confined to the internal world. You just assume it because science and logic tell you so."

As always, neither side is able to convince the other. The war continues to wage itself, and I live as a tumultuous battleground.

The unresolved conflict between my logical and creative sides pervades everything I do, believe, and am. I love the poetic and descriptive power of words. I enjoy nothing more than flurries of figurativeness. Playing with the power of these words and altering them is one of my specialties. Still, I am often the strict grammarian, who organizes his prepositions and distinguishes between the dash and the

colon. He is not concerned with flow or flower, only syntax and punctuation. In physics, I am the scientist; momentum is mass times velocity and everything is composed of atoms. In a field, gazing at the sun as it descends through the trees, I feel, I know that I am not the components of a rock rearranged. Beethoven, I am aware, composed impeccably, and for his perfection I salute him. Mozart, however, despite his theoretical shortcomings, affects me more deeply and sincerely. I can criticize his composition, but I can never suppress the intense feeling his music stirs within me.

The result of being pulled in both directions is that I am characterized by a certain chaos. Far from harming me, my chaotic nature is the source of my individuality. Somehow, my conflicting sides benefit each other even as they battle each other. The logician within me ensures that my writing is clear and grammatically correct; the creatician adds flavor and originality. Without logic, I could not use science and the conventions of philosophy, and without merging logic with creativity, I would be unable to develop my own uniquely chaotic deviations. I am chaos incarnate, but the chaos works.

✎   ✎   ✎

Essay No. 7
[Attached to the following essay was a piece of paper with the following handwritten words: "Great organization. You rock and sway to the point of making your audience seasick."]

I still wonder why I kept this debate judge's ballot from the first time I competed in expository speaking. It's not as if those comments bring back fond memories of overwhelming success. Apparently, the hand gestures I so desperately tried to include, combined with a constant shifting back and forth on my feet, produced an effect quite different from the one I had intended to achieve. I didn't even belong up there, anyway. An experienced debater, well-versed in the art of speaking on the spur of the moment, I had crossed over into the realm of rehearsed speech, a place which *"true"* debaters classified as infinitely inferior. Yet despite this, I still cannot deny it: speech and debate together constitute

the activity that is most meaningful for what they have shown me about myself.

When I first started debating, it was as if I had found a different person inside of me. Like Dr. Jekyll and Mr. Hyde, I would transform from a normally quiet and reserved young man into a frenzied speaker whose words came out so fast they bordered on unintelligible. The pressure of each round stripped away my inhibitions, leaving nothing standing between me and victory. After a year of experiencing the thrill of arguing against fellow debaters, I entered expository speaking to occupy the time in-between debate rounds. As I soon discovered, "Mr. Hyde" would not work for speech competitions since the speed and argumentation of debate are not compatible with the composure and presentation needed for speech. Despite some initial setbacks, I continued participating and in turn, soon realized that I could be calm and rational while speaking at length on a chosen topic instead of tense and critical or shy and tentative.

Strange as it may seem, I sometimes think that I must have multiple personalities or else I would never get through a debate tournament. From nervously waiting for a round to begin to urgently appealing a judge to consider my arguments to projecting confidence and authority during a speech, public speaking has brought out many different sides of me. While these vast extremes may lead one to think that I need immediate psychological help, I remain grateful for learning that I am not confined to be only "one" person. And perhaps that is why I did not throw away that ballot in disgust. It represents the surfacing of yet another aspect of my personality, one I am proud of . . . even if it does make people seasick.

✎   ✎   ✎

MEANINGFUL METAPHORS AND SYMBOLIC KEEPSAKES *(6 Essays)*

Essay No. 8

When I was in the eighth grade, my backpack disappeared from my life. I can't remember what happened to it. I may have lost it, or perhaps my

sister took it. Anyway, I found myself backpackless. I need a backpack to carry all my books, binders, pens, pencils, highlighters, protractors, calculators and compasses (sometimes I go a bit overboard with the tools I bring to class). I began to use this strange pack of my dad's, which was actually more like a soft-sided briefcase with back-straps. That pack was truly the ugliest piece of luggage I have ever seen. It embarrassed my friends and made me feel like a fool, but I had no choice but to wear it. I couldn't find any alternative where I lived in Saudi Arabia, so I promptly ordered a backpack from L.L. Bean.

I really enjoy pouring over catalogs, so I enthusiastically decided on the nine-inch deep L.L. Bean Deluxe (I need a roomy backpack). For the color, I debated among eggplant, forest green, pine, and the other excitedly-named shades, but eventually decided on mallard blue. It was a shade of blue that bordered on iridescent. I knew no one else would have a backpack that color. I sent off my order form and eagerly waited.

It takes a few months for L.L. Bean to get something all the way to Saudi Arabia, but my backpack eventually arrived. I realized that mallard blue had been a bold choice. The color could definitely be called ugly, and its brightness could not be denied. It was also huge, especially on my eighth-grade body. The crowning detail was my initials "H-A-W" embroidered on the back. Yes, it spells "haw." However, it was clearly an improvement over Dad's dork-case. I loved it, and it has since gone with me everywhere.

My bag has acquired a great deal of character since eighth grade. There are little marks and scratches all over the material. There's a small sparkly bead flower I sewed on once in a fit of procrastination; the flower was originally accompanied by a diagonal line of sparkly beads above the reflective strip on the bag, but I decided that was just too much and removed the line of beads. One can faintly see where I wrote "excess" on the bag. I don't know why I wrote that; I just went through a phase when I thought "excess" was a cool word. Also on the bag is leftover stitching from where I had attached a Saudi Arabian flag, which I removed because I feared it made me vulnerable to terrorist attacks. On the back pocket, I added a patch proclaiming me to be an "advanced" diver from the scuba class I took during the summer. When I have time, I plan to add another patch from NOLS, the National Outdoor Leadership School,

where I spent part of my summer. The final touch is a little guardian angel pin that my aunt gave to me. It looks silly in it's shiny golden newness next to the rest of my rugged ragged bag, but I could think of no better place for the pin, which I'm supposed to keep near me at all times.

I think my backpack is a good representation of me. Just like my backpack, my personality is full of random, loud elements that don't really make sense together. Their only unifying force is the fact that they all belong to me, so I like them. Just as my backpack has picked up a patch here and a beaded design there, I have picked up ideas here and insights there throughout our travels together. It records my history more personally than a diary ever could, and although I know it is just a material object, I would be at a loss if I were ever to lose it.

✎   ✎   ✎

Essay No. 9

Spaceships, fireboats, castles, trucks, and pirate ships are just a handful of the countless projects I have constructed throughout my childhood. No, I was not some child prodigy enveloped in the world of construction. I just had an undying passion for a tiny piece of molded plastic. I went through many toy phases as I progressed from pre-kindergarten through eighth grade, but the toys that I have always come back to are the ones that can become something different every time I use them: the Lego building blocks.

My original exposure to the world of Lego was at the age of five. I remember fondly the younger brother of the Lego, the Duplo. Duplo blocks were generally much larger and simpler than Lego blocks. An entire car could be made from five or six Duplo blocks. After graduating out of Duplos, I entered the amazing world of Legos. From that point on I accumulated quite a collection of Legos, enough to fill four massive crates.

My pride and joy was a lunar base I designed that covered nearly four square feet of my room. I played with it constantly and I continued to add to it until one dark day when my good friend Andy fell on the base during a vicious pillow fight, completely destroying the whole thing. Andy and I are still good friends, but I will never forgive him for demolishing my prized possession.

Legos have had an immeasurable effect on my life. They shaped my childhood, and as a result, they have also shaped me into the person I am today. My development is strangely parallel to that of the development of any Lego project. Every Lego project begins with an assortment of pieces, all different shapes and colors. Some pieces I find to be essential to the project, while others can be discarded. I always start with a basic foundation. From that point, I build up and out until it is no longer a set of random blocks. It has taken shape and has become something that now has its own identity. My life began with exposure to a variety of experiences, and throughout my childhood, I learned to develop my values based on all these different experiences. Eventually, a form began to emerge that distinguished me from everyone else.

Legos may not have changed the world the way the airplane and the computer have, but for one little boy, they accomplished what no incredible piece of technology could do. They released an unstoppable flow of imagination and curiosity that has shaped the boy into a creative, energetic, and confident young man.

✎   ✎   ✎

Essay No. 10

If each person's life could be likened to a book, the early chapters of mine would be some of the fullest. For more than six years, I was a partaker of the pageantry of European history and culture. My childhood in Munich, Germany, and my travels throughout the continent have shaped me in countless ways. I want to share with you one small chapter of my life which took place in Florence, Italy, where I became acquainted with a man named David.

His sheer immensity is what I remember most, a mute giant whose face said a thousand words, a marble god brought forth by the worshipping artist. From above, a gray-blue nimbus flowed from the skylight, not reflecting or refracting but rather rippling and gliding, becoming part of his silken mane and sinewy limbs.

I reached out my child's hand, plump with life, and brushed his ashen toe. There was a violent collision of the real and the fantastic, the breathing human being and the living art. I raised my eyes to his, and

mine were locked in their embrace, knowing that they would never turn away. I set my palm flat against his pedestal, I was entranced by the cool warmth of the stone. David, with your fleeting frown and casual pose . . . how did you have the courage to fight mighty Goliath? Ah, but how could a seven-year-old girl see him thus, you say. It is the seventeen-year-old who now knows what I saw that day—human potential in its purest form.

Michelangelo captured not a moment but a lifetime. Never have I stood or will I stand again in such awe of life itself. Glancing back, alone, in the softly falling dust motes, I knew. I knew the greatness of man, and I am filled with its marble weight even now.

✎   ✎   ✎

Essay No. 11

I hate contact paper. You know, the paper with flowery designs on one side and impossibly sticky glue on the other; the kind that pastes to the shelves in the cabinets. You'd understand my dislike—no, extreme hatred—if you've ever had to paper thirty-five shelves, twenty-eight drawers, ten boxes, and a partridge in a pear tree. Not only is it four days of back-breaking work, it is pure torture trying to make the paper cooperate. Perhaps a quick lesson on how I paper shelves would be enlightening:

(1) First, I figure out the amount of contact paper I need. Although the paper manufacturer thoughtfully placed measured intervals on the back of the paper, the carpenter "conveniently" created the shelves somewhat unevenly, measuring sixteen-point-two inches by twenty-point-three inches. Of course, now those nifty lines on the back of the contact paper have no use due to the "artistic liberty" of a carpenter who would not recognize a ruler if shown one. So what am I to do? Thinking rationally, I derive a simple equation to compute the exact quantity required. All I need to know is, oh, basic calculus.

(2) Next, I separate the paper from the backing. This is where I undergo vigorous exercise. The enterprise that produces this paper leaves a minuscule half-millimeter of space in which to jam my fingernail, in my torturous effort to separate them. However, I have found that by

holding the paper between my legs, with one hand firmly gasping the actual contact paper, the other hand grabbing the backing, and by jumping up and down (in the same manner as squeezing into jeans after the holiday season), I should be able to finish that process in, oh say, ten minutes. (My record is nine minutes and forty-four seconds.)

(3) Now that the papers are finally separated, I reluctantly perform the most tedious part. This part appears to be relatively simple: I put the paper, sticky side down, on the shelf. Unfortunately, life is just not that considerate. This paper has crazy glue on the back. If it gets caught on a table top, to itself, to the door, to your hair, or to your brother, it's going to stay there. Trust me (my brother wouldn't speak to me for a week since the paper is waterproof). As for the paper on the shelf, I need to put it down exactly where I want it to be; a slight miscalculation of the eye creates a wrinkle that is permanent.

So much for enlightenment. What's my point? Well, contact paper is similar to my way of relating to people (ah-hah!). Note the similarities:

(1) First, like figuring out the amount of contact paper, I have to find the group of people I am most like. Usually, everyone is kind enough to present me with a brief overview of his or her life (a.k.a., facade) that seems perfect and evenly made. I, however, do not fit in with these "flawless" people. I have that extra three-quarter inches on my hips . . . and in my personality. I'm a little offbeat and a bit eccentric; belonging to the "norm" is calculus to me.

(2) Trying to get to know people away from the cliques that formed in middle school is vigorous exercise. These people are attached like glue to their childhood ideas, and they refuse to let go of their prehistoric rituals. In my adolescent effort to gain acceptance, I undergo various physical transformations. Hence, the squeezing myself into the too-tight jeans.

(3) Even though I think I have finally found that circle of friends, I often come upon the discovery that I have a million other obstacles to hurdle. And in the case of humans, one mistake might become an everlasting wrinkle in our relationship.

Looking back, the search for my niche has not been that horrible. Even though I have not been able to find the precise clique in which to belong, I have met a variety of people. This diversity of personalities have helped broaden my horizons and experiences. Though there have

been difficult times, the end result of a cultured and multifaceted background has been well worth the obstacles. After all, it's the social bumps and bruises that create a distinct, mature character; social pressures have humanized me much the same way geological pressure turns coal into diamonds.

So it's not surprising that I have discovered that contact paper isn't that bad—when used for the right purpose. In a recent meeting of the March of Dimes Chain Reaction Youth Council, we made grief boxes. Grief boxes are for mothers whose babies are stillborn or die during birth. The council makes the boxes and the hospital puts in the baby's birth certificate, death certificate, and a baby blanket. We made the grief parcels by taking regular shoe boxes and covering the box and lid with pretty contact paper. Then we glued white flannel around the inside, and added lace around the top with a ribbon bow. Very touching and thoughtful. For once, I was not upset about all the tedious work created by the contact paper. I was really glad that I would be able to make a grieving mother's day a little brighter. Maybe I don't hate contact paper. Maybe I just thought I did.

✎   ✎   ✎

Essay No. 12

I own a diamond so small that you have to look closely to distinguish it from its base. Surrounding the mineral is a thin line of gold forming the shape of a Jewish star. A gold chain holds the star and when you place it around your neck, you have to be careful that the diamond side faces forward.

I was fourteen years old when I found it wrapped up in tissue paper, awaiting my return from the synagogue. A small piece of paper had been ripped and folded to make a card which read: "Congratulations on your Bat-Mitzvah. Love, Dad." That is all my father had to say. He drove up from his Christian home to enter my Jewish world, leaving his new family of three to join his old family of four. He watched as I was accepted into the world of Jewish adults. I valued the necklace only because it was the first time in seven years my dad and mom came together without screaming or causing tears. Thus, it becomes a charm of good luck.

The necklace stayed clasped around my neck twenty-four hours a day and eventually traveled with me to Israel. I held it in my hands for a sense of protection as I flew out of San Francisco and held it once again as I landed on foreign ground. For six weeks, my thoughts kept returning to home and to the security of not worrying about daily acts of violence between two peoples fighting for one piece of land. When I mistakenly entered the Arab side of the Wailing Wall, it seemed as though my necklace grew large and those who looked in my direction saw only the small star that hung from my neck. My hand reached to hold it as I quickly left their place of reverence, squeezing the star so that it made indentations on my fingers. I only pressed harder until my feet led me back to the Jewish side of the white stones that make up the Wailing Wall. My necklace brought me strength and the harder I pressed my fingers against it, the more secure I felt.

While the shape of my star stayed the same, the shape of my life took off in many directions. I still wore my necklace, but always over my required uniform of the Papa Murphy's Pizza shirt and apron. Tomato paste and oil splattered onto the chain and occasionally onto the stone. One evening, an irritable old man came in near closing. As I took his order, I noticed that he too wore a Star of David. I started a conversation meant to last seconds that turned into ten minutes. We talked of voyages to Israel, Rabbis that made us question, and my distaste for parsley and salt at Passover Seders. I left work that night and walked in the cold air caressing my star with a sense of connection, a feeling of closeness to the people of my faith.

I cautiously placed my necklace around my neck as I once again boarded a plane to leave for Jonquiere, Quebec. For the following six weeks, I studied in a country where few people knew of the Jewish religion, and where those who looked at my necklace noticed it only for its beauty. Classmates in my courses knew of Judaism solely through stereotypes from television. For many, I was the first Jew they had met. I spoke less of my faith as a Jew, yet noticed its impact on me more. My necklace was my identity. I pulled it from underneath my shirt and placed it on the outside of my clothing, not caring if the diamond side faced forward.

✎   ✎   ✎

Essay No. 13

"Have you ever noticed that the people never rip the paper off their gifts? The boxes are rigged so that the lid will simply lift off." Some time after sharing this insight with my friend Jennifer, I received a birthday present from her wrapped in such a way that the top came off without tearing the blue paper. I kept the special box and placed my birthday cards in it along with a few other letters I regarded as treasures. Since then, I've moved across the country twice, but the box remains on the top shelf of my closet, now joined by two other shoe boxes, a pink, heart-shaped container, and a hand-woven Guatemalan bag—all overflowing with the letters that chronicle so much of my life and so many of my friendships.

My inability to part with any of my letters—from the shortest note from Grandma to one of the hundreds of letters from my friend Melissa—cannot be easily explained. Certainly the love letters play upon my conceit, gently building my fragile teenage self esteem. Beyond these, however, lie the babbling prose of girlfriends, the one note I received from my camp roommate, and the letter accompanying the black and white photo of John, Paul, George, and Ringo which I won in the "Eight Days a Week" Beatles sweepstakes. I treasure each of these and hold tight the history locked within them in my changing world; to quote the opening of one of Melissa's letters, "Life is so wonderful, and so unfair, and so confusing."

Throughout my life, I have clung to any concrete portion of the world I could get my hands on, and I have developed a deep trust in, and yearning for, the written word. Unlike spoken words, written words have a timelessness; they hold a promise forever, and they bind the writer to his promise indelibly. Smashed between a slumber party invitation and a post card from Florida, my great grandmother will always be waiting "with love" inside a card decorated with lavender flowers. When someday I get married, my first boyfriend will still miss my "soft voice and soft eyes." I rarely need to check these reminders that I can never stop being loved, being a friend, and making a difference in the lives of others. I am always conscious of the gathering that awaits me in the dusty boxes. Each time I receive a new letter, I carefully place it into the little life museum perched on my closet shelf.

FAMILY TIES *(5 Essays)*

Essay No. 14

I did not appreciate her nightly ritual until I had grown taller than she. And it was even longer before I remembered that my first memories of her included the familiar sounds and smells which escaped from her kitchen each night. As she labors, her husband reads the day's Chinese newspaper, while down the hall her American daughter studies. Tonight, however, things are changing. Tonight her daughter is not so American.

I sit with my mother at the dining table and learn to make sushi for the first time. Not the Japanese kind with raw fish, but my mother's own creation. I first add rice vinegar and sugar to the just-cooked rice, mixing with the rice paddle. Spreading the rice on lightly-toasted nori, I pile on shreds of dried pork. On impulse, I decide to add in some octopus. When at last I am ready to roll the sushi, my mother is twinkling with soundless laughter, for my fingers, and even my shirt, are spotted with grains of sticky white rice.

I must hold the sushi firmly, then press down and roll; soon I find my own rhythm. My sushi-making surprises my parents, since they see me only as the daughter who refused to attend a second year of Chinese school, the child who no longer speaks Mandarin or Taiwanese.

Tonight I extend my arms across the ocean that separates my parents from me. I try to make up for the silent dinners and the stereotypes we cast on each other. My parents do not hear my words, just as I am sometimes deaf to theirs. They buy McDonald's for me, though I hate fast food. Even tonight—this attempt to get closer to my mother—is viewed as an aberration; they do not understand why I would care to make sushi. I fear that this attempt, and every one after tonight, will ultimately fail. I am, every day, moving away from my parents, and I walk these streets that are foreign to them but home to me. I cannot mend the ropes which tore with my first word of English, the ropes which had begun to strain years ago at my first step. Though my parents may try, they do not define me. I am my own creator.

Still, I will try again another day, with impossible hopes that we can make a lasting connection. Now, for a little while, I listen to my mother tell me her childhood stories, and I unfold parts of myself.

These few hundred words are only a sliver of the entire me; you have tasted only a sprinkling of the ingredients in my sushi. If you wait, you will taste not only my cold cucumbers and my octopus, but also my words and thoughts swimming around your taste buds.

✎   ✎   ✎

Essay No. 15

"He looks like Old Man Winter," my friend Mark said, looking at a picture of my grandfather, whose steel-white mustache and thinning wisps around his mostly bald scalp gave off a sense of warm wisdom and beneficence. In the picture he is holding my two-year-old cousin and because of that he smiles in happiness. "Is he the one who takes you skiing?"

"Yeah," I answered, "he taught me how to ski."

"Wow, cool guy."

Stubborn, sometimes miserly but often grandly generous, my grandfather has been one of the greatest positive influences in my life, and he is one of my few heroes. Though he did not always get along with his three daughters, he is definitely one of the greats in the eyes of his five grandchildren.

When I was two he bought a ski house in New Hampshire in order to teach his grandchildren to ski, having learned himself only five years earlier. At age five I was taken out to the mountain and, under my grandfather's instruction, was soon the terror of the bunny slope.

When I was eight, he put me on the tennis court with an oversized wooden racket in my hands, and proceeded to teach me the basics of the game, a game that he had himself learned only in his fifties. Over the past few summers, as I taught tennis at the camp at my school, I found his words coming out through my lips: "Keep your racket back, your eyes on the ball, and follow through." It has taken me this long to realize how much my grandfather has taught me. At eight years old it seemed natural to me that every time I went to my grandparents' house, he would take me to the Boston Science Museum and explain the latest exhibit. On the swan boats in the Public Gardens he would tell stories of the dangerous hospital ship he served on in World War II. I looked forward

to long trips with him to Beth Israel Hospital for treatment of his psoriasis, even though when we got to the hospital I would have to sit in the car, looking out for the meter maid with a handful of change.

My grandfather was as well known for taking all his grandchildren out for tennis and a movie as he was for bringing the salesman at the Toyota dealership to the verge of tears, trying to cut a deal. He is as happy playing his violin as he is sitting down with a big bowl of chocolate ice cream. He taught me, above all else, that if there is something you want to do, there is a way to do it. His life is that story. Even though now, at 78, because of a bad knee he might not be able to play tennis or take me skiing as much as he'd like, he still sets the example for his grandchildren and teaches the lesson and that he has all along: never stop learning.

✎ ✎ ✎

Essay No. 16

I keep remembering odd things: the way she loved daffodils, her delight at the antics of our dog, jokes she told at the dinner table, her subtle brand of feminism, the look in her eyes when she talked about my future. I knew about college before I'd ever heard of high school; I was Mom's second chance at the degree she never had.

Her parents pushed her too much, too hard, too fast, and she always wished she hadn't let the pressure overwhelm her. She dropped out of college after one semester for marriage and a secretarial job. While she never regretted marrying my father, she always regretted giving up her dream of becoming an accountant. She was determined her eldest daughter would never miss an opportunity, and she missed out on so many herself so I could succeed.

She was the one person I could talk to about anything: politics, dating, parties, failed tests, or nail polish. She was right about so much, so often—much more than I gave her credit for at the time. We never did agree on clothes. She favored the J. Crew look, I kept trying for (and failing at) the neo-sixties style. One year we didn't buy any new clothes at all in a battle of wills: she refused to buy anything that didn't "fit me properly" and I refused to wear anything with an alligator on it.

She loved the holidays, Christmas most of all. One of the most intensely special times of my life was Christmas my sophomore year, when I played Tiny Tim in a local community theater production of "A Christmas Carol." Mom delighted in my endless rehearsal stories and spent hours helping me work out ways of disguising my long hair. There's a line in the show: "And it was always said of him that he knew how to keep Christmas well, if any man alive possessed the knowledge." Change the pronouns and that quote describes Mom perfectly.

I never imagined she wouldn't be here now, micro-managing, debating the merits of such-and-such college with me, chasing the dog around the living room, ruining spaghetti, explaining "power colors," and relishing exciting changes in IRS forms. I never thought cancer could strike so quickly, could kill someone so strong and determined in only a year.

She's the one person I couldn't imagine living without; now, since last January, I've had to. Suddenly, I have no one to talk to about meaningless little things, no one whose advice I trust implicitly to help me with decisions. When I come home from school, I come home to an empty house, haunted by memories of the year she spent here dying. I remember the disastrous Thanksgiving when she was nauseous and delusional, our wonderful last Christmas Eve together, the tangle of tubes in the family room, the needlepoint picture of Rainbow Row she labored over while stuck in bed, and the bags of M&Ms she always kept within reach.

What I feel cheated of is the future we'll never have.

Essay No. 17

He was the best of brothers; he was the worst of brothers. Unfortunately, he was the worst—for a long time before I thought otherwise. In short, Mike did not fit my image of the ideal older brother. He was not a friend. Instead, he was my enemy, my nightmare, a bully from whom I could not escape. Just the thought of our horrible childhood encounters makes me cringe.

I can recall the nightly "pounding sessions" that left me screaming for my parents, and my parents screaming at Mike. In fact, it seemed as

though they were always focused on my brother, usually for something he had done wrong. My friends' older brothers were their mentors, their protectors, their idols. Not mine. The only interaction we had consisted of physical and verbal abuse. Needless to say, there was not much affection between us.

I can't remember exactly when I discovered I was smarter than my brother, but it was early on and it afforded me the chance to gain at least the intellectual edge. I took great delight in bringing home better grades, beating him at family games, and winning our verbal encounters. I usually paid the price, but at least my pride stayed somewhat intact.

Two winters ago, my family took a ski vacation to Colorado. Many of our school friends were there, as well. We skied, we ate, we partied. I tried to avoid Mike as best I could, but when we were together, he never missed an opportunity to torment me, especially in front of the others.

One particularly frigid morning found my brother, a mutual friend, and me perched tentatively (at least I was) atop a narrow, plunging slope. Trees lined both sides, and the sun had yet to make any impact on the ice-encrusted snow. Mike went first. He made two turns, lost his balance, and began to career downhill, clearly out of control. Our eyes widened as we saw him veer left and disappear into the forest. "Mike!" we screamed several times. There was no sound.

I could feel a churning sensation in my stomach as we quickly made our way down to the spot where we had last seen my brother. The forest was dense and dark, and it swallowed our frantic cries without reply. I had already kicked off my skis and begun to tread through deep snow in the direction of Mike's tracks when I saw him. He lay motionless between two trees, and I was sure he was dead.

"Get a doctor!" I pleaded with our friend. As he skied away, I approached my brother, terrified. "Mike," I repeated several times as I stared at the bloody scrape above his left eye. He did not respond, but I was almost sure he was breathing. I knew not to move him, and the only thing I could think to do was keep him warm until help arrived. I lay at his side and tried to cover as much of him with my body as possible without any weight.

That's when my mind began to race. I had wished him dead so many times and now that it seemed a distinct possibility, somehow I felt

responsible. I was actually afraid that it might happen, and feelings began to surface that had been lost or repressed for as long as I could remember. My whole body heaved and shook. As I found myself praying for Mike's life, I began to question my role in our relationship. In my mind I had always been the "victim," the innocent object of his wrath. I had never accepted any responsibility for our lack of closeness, but suddenly I realized that I had played a major part as well. I was a master at infuriating Mike; I knew the right "buttons to push" and enjoyed seeing him and my parents fight. I delighted in the frustration Mike felt when I brought home scholastic awards and straight A's. My brother was the perfect foil; and in some twisted way I actually owed him a great deal, for he was the inspiration for much of my motivation and success, a reverse role model.

Suddenly I didn't seem so innocent, I had used Mike as he had used me, and our relationship was the real victim. I truly felt compassion for him and wondered if this new and strange sensation was "brotherly love." As it turned out, Mike had a concussion, no broken bones, and had to sit out the rest of our vacation in bed. I finished the week a slightly better skier and a brother who had found a new level of understanding about accepting responsibility, and one who had rediscovered some long-forgotten emotions.

A year and a half later I am happy to report that our relationship is much improved. We still don't have a great deal in common, but we do have a newfound respect for each another; and although we still bicker and fight, I sense a growing connection between us. Mike called home from college last week and asked to speak with me. We actually had a meaningful conversation, and it felt wonderful.

Essay No. 18

All eyes were focused on me. This was it. The tension had been building up to this point, and I knew there was no way out. I had gotten myself into this predicament, and I was the only one that could get myself out of it. There was nobody to turn to, for they were all waiting for my final move. I had never felt so alone, so isolated.

I thumbed through my cards for the fourth consecutive time, and I could still not decide which one to throw. I glanced up from my cards and caught a glimpse of each player. I immediately felt the intensity of my brother's eyes glaring at me from across the table. He did not provide me with the support and reassurance I was looking for from my partner. I shifted my eyes to the right. My mother, having just discarded a five of clubs and seeing that it was of no use to me, was sipping coffee with a carefree grin of relief. Then I peered directly at the most intimidating canasta player I have ever encountered. Great Grandma Rose was calmly humming a tuneless tune which added to her enigma. As this crafty eighty-eight year old lady squinted at her cards through her bifocals, I knew that time was running out; I had to make my decision. The most obvious choice was to discard the king of spades for which I had no use, but I was afraid that she was waiting for this card. My alternative was to break up my meld and throw the six of clubs, a card which I felt somewhat safe in throwing.

In the midst of my despair, great grandma delivered the final blow. She stopped humming and uttered these dreaded words: "It only hurts for a minute."

She could not have dug a knife any deeper. My brother's eyes were flaring with tension, I had complete control over his fate, and I knew our team unity was riding on the outcome of my decision. I therefore decided to play defensively and throw the six of clubs. No sooner had my discard settled on top of the pile than my great grandmother's hand darted out to snatch up the stack of cards and my brother simultaneously belted out a scream. "The six of clubs? How could you throw the six of clubs!"

I wanted to ask him if the king of spades would have been any better, but I knew a rebuttal was useless. I knew he would get over it soon enough, and like Grandma Rose says, "It only hurts for minute!"

After my great grandma laid down her meld and sorted her cards, the game continued (and so did her humming). Although we lost that particular hand, my brother and I miraculously came back to snatch victory from the jaws of defeat. As we reveled in our triumph (my brother had now forgiven me for discarding the six of clubs), I could not resist directing my newly acquired quote at our opponents, who were mulling over their defeat. "Well, I have only one thing to say." My smile

was so big that I could feel my cheeks stretching. "It only hurts for a minute."

Although my great grandmother had no intention of being profound, this quote actually embodies an important concept. Many people spend so much time worrying about the infinite possibilities that may result from any decision they make that they actually never make a decision at all. Although it is necessary to weigh the options and consider various viewpoints, excessive deliberation can often be detrimental. From personal experience, I have found it is usually better to think about the choices and come to a firm decision rather than to prolong the problem and perhaps create a new one by avoiding a commitment one way or the other. The best course of action is to make the wisest choice possible with the available information and then to make the most out of your initial decision. Even if in retrospect you see a better alternative, you can always pursue a new direction based on what you have learned through this experience. Surprisingly, what may at first appear to be failure may often spark an unforeseen success. I have learned not to let undue hesitation hinder my ability to take advantage of opportunities. After all, as my great grandmother so eloquently remarked during those heated canasta games, "It only hurts for a minute!"

✎   ✎   ✎

TERRIFIC TEACHERS *(4 Essays)*

Essay No. 19

"Breez in and breez out. Clear yor mind by zinking of somezing plasant." For five minutes, all of us found ourselves sitting cross-legged on the floor with a soft, sleepy look on our faces as we subconsciously nodded to the soothing rhythmic voice of our French teacher. Our heads were still half wafting in the delicious swirls of dreamland, barely dwelling in the bittersweet shock of reality. Time whizzed by swiftly and we were forced to tend to the grueling task of untangling our aching frames, stiffened from prolonged straining positions.

Madame DuPont would then launch into her lesson plan for the day with much animation. She often exuded boundless vitality and seemed to

bounce with every step she took, while the rest of us were just starting to recover from the morning blues. I imagined her to be another Napoleon Bonaparte, seeking to instill in us a certain form of discipline as she led us in the formidable mission of conquering the French language.

As we tried hopelessly to mimic her genuine Parisian accent, she would persistently encourage us by dictating, "Errrroll yor Rrrrr's *messieurs* et *mesdemolselles*! You must enunciate yor vowels and consonants properly! . . . *Oui*, zat's it!" Whenever we succeeded in our strenuous efforts, she would reward us with her trademark impish grin. The sight of her lively expression often led our hearts to be consoled with instant relief and a true sense of achievement. Her optimistic attitude toward life itself proved to be highly contagious, for it made us even more susceptible to learning. Our steadfast attentions never failed to drift away to the soporific world of daydreams, designated in our minds as No Man's Land. The mystic ambiance she generated from her manner and her unique style of teaching was somehow bewitching. Whether she was instructing us in the conjugation of *savoir* or assisting us in differentiating between the usage of *avoir* and *être* in relation to other verbs, she always did it *avec beaucoup de plaisir*. She was a special individual who would help others without request and who was willing to listen to people's problems without prejudice. In her I found a role model as well as a friend who I could depend on.

She firmly believed the path to successful learning was to make sure the materials presented were enlightening yet intriguing and never too tedious. I was always amazed at how she was able to arouse in us such an enduring interest in French. This enigma perplexed me, and I vowed to unveil her secret one day. I did not get the opportunity to discover her formula for success, for she moved away soon after I made the pledge to myself. However, not long after her departure I received an unexpected letter from her that satisfied my lingering curiosity. Within its content, I realized what I had been searching for had been there since the very first day I walked into her class. It was the self-confidence she possessed and the staunch belief that she could make a difference that made her a lasting success in my mind.

✎　　✎　　✎

Essay No. 20

If the lesson of life is happiness, then I have met the most dramatic of teachers. By the world's standards, my "teacher's" words are far from eloquent, his style far from graceful, his works far from wondrous. Yet in his determination and courage I see a hero, a hero unlike those we normally choose. He is Patrick, and, by the way, he has Down Syndrome.

Working as the dance and movement specialist during the summer of 1994 at Carousel Farm, a summer camp for mentally challenged and neurologically impaired children, has shown me what true goodness really is. Pure souls do exist, and Patrick is one of them. Patrick did not see the differences of skin color among his camp friends or notice that Jimmy came to camp every day wearing the same unwashed clothes. He kissed and hugged everyone just the same and flirtatiously called everyone "boo-tiful." Patrick had the talent of savoring the flavor of each and every moment. No time was wasted with the words "I can't," but rather "We're done already?" He didn't simply come to camp. He *lived* camp. I marveled at his unending energy and his zest for fun.

The "Incredible Hulk" (as he liked to call himself) and I shared a special friendship those unforgettable eight weeks. I taught him the "Electric Slide" and he proudly presented me with hand-picked dandelions each morning. He treasured the shiny star stickers I gave him for being a super dancer. We shared potato chips under the trees at lunch time. Through the sweaty days and the not-so-fun rainy days, we learned from each other. I gave Patrick the feeling that he was wonderful and loved, while he taught me to laugh at the happy and colorful moments that usually flash by without a thought—a kickball game with good friends, the tickle of a horse's whiskers on your cheek, or a piggyback ride in the pool. Patrick had a jack-o-lantern smile for every occasion.

Contrary to the world's standards, I say that Patrick's words really are eloquent. After all, who else could respond to my statement, "I love you very much" with "How many 'verys'?" Every female at camp can surely attest to his unmatched style and charm. His works—the home run in softball, the pencil can in arts and crafts, the "Chicken Dance" lead in our dance finale—were wondrous too, because they were challenges that

Patrick met with just a little extra effort. Just a little extra effort, that's all. Way to go, Patrick.

I won't see Patrick until Open House during next year's camp season. We are separated by many miles and find ourselves in two different worlds during the school year. Yet Patrick is with me, inside my head and heart. Sensitive and able to see the decency in everyone, he has touched me and changed me. If the lesson of life is happiness, then I surely have met the most inspiring of teachers. Patrick has taught me to erase the preceding "if."

Essay No. 21

I felt like a cadet at West Point that first week of fifth grade. Mrs. Stith was our sergeant, commanding us to "stand at attention," "walk single file," "keep heads up" and "speak only when spoken to." We had only two rules to obey in her classroom: never talk while Mrs. Stith is talking, and do your homework! We did not dare break these rules, fearing an arduous obstacle course to climb as our consequence or a firing squad awaiting Mrs. Stith's command to release an arsenal of bullets into our bodies.

My fifth-grade mind was not accustomed to such a demanding teacher. Coloring outside the lines, reading *The Great Adventures of Encyclopedia Brown* and building mobiles with construction paper had been the norm. My mouth gaped at the sight of endless reading packets and workbook pages. I was in boot camp now and Mrs. Stith was going to toughen up the troops. Mrs. Stith could see our agony, our pleading eyes hoping she would blow her whistle and let us take a break from the work. But she yelled at the class at any sign of softness. Twenty pages of reading every night kept our stamina up. I cried at the thought of learning how to spell "dictionary," "miserable" and "criminal." I sweated over decimals. How could I learn all this and still have time to watch *Cosby*? This wasn't a youngster's usual anxiety. I honestly thought I hated Mrs. Stith, or "Mrs. Stiff," as we called her, snickering as we pictured our gray-haired tyrant being lowered into a tomb. Who did this old woman think she was anyway, always barking at the class? I had always been the

teacher's pet. "Is my work not good enough?" I wondered. How could she destroy my confidence so easily?

"Carrie, how could you get this question wrong?"

"I . . . I . . . don't know," I managed, lowering my head in shame, unable to look at Mrs. Stith's disappointed face.

"Don't you know what a preposition is?"

"Yes, Mrs. Stith," I replied, knowing that this blunder meant K.P. duty. I would have to study my composition book a little extra tonight.

I can't pinpoint exactly why, but sometime during those first few weeks I decided to study hard and make Mrs. Stith proud of me. Maybe I dreamed of following in my older brother's prominent footsteps (some thought they were left by Bigfoot). I wanted to be as studious and intelligent as Christopher. I couldn't destroy the name that my brother and I had established. Mediocrity wasn't part of my vocabulary. I had always been the best in class, favored by my teachers and often chosen to read aloud or go to the chalkboard to do multiplication tables. The difference was that now it didn't come so easily. I would have to work.

Two-page reports turned into detailed posters explaining the formation of igneous, metamorphic, and sedimentary rocks. Mrs. Stith noticed her students' best efforts and rewarded us for hard work with smelly stickers. We loved those stickers and hung them on the wall. One could easily discern my long trail of grapes, strawberries and apples. Reading packets became enjoyable. I left the world of Ramona Quimby and discovered Miss Havisham's mansion, the plummeting guillotine and Jacob Marley's rattling chains. That year marked the beginning of my battle with the nerd syndrome.

Fifth grade helped establish my reputation as a brain. I would skip recess and stay after school just to talk with Mrs. Stith. I would spend hours every night studying beyond the assigned homework. I didn't mind if other kids laughed at me for being studious; they just hadn't met the *real* Mrs. Stith. I no longer saw her as a rigid drill sergeant but rather, a helpful platoon leader. For my part, I was no longer a raw recruit but well on my way to becoming a skilled soldier.

What, in the beginning, were tears of fright and frustration turned to tears of sorrow when I graduated from fifth grade. For graduation Mrs. Stith gave me a special gift—a copy of *A Day No Pigs Would Die*. She

wrote on the back cover: "I loved this book. I hope you will too. You are an outstanding girl. Best of luck always. Love, Mrs. Stith." Mrs. Stith retired that year and I never saw my friend again.

✎   ✎   ✎

Essay No. 22

"Suppose for a moment that I am out walking my beagle and she jumps into the Farmington River down near the bridge and begins to swim across it." Pausing for a moment to allow the class to picture his feeble, obedient beagle escaping from him, Mr. Joffray, affectionately known as "Joff," begins Calculus class. "Now my beagle, being roughly the same age as I, cannot swim very quickly. In fact, she can only swim as fast as the Farmington River's current—about one meter per second. She wants to swim across the Farmington River and end up directly opposite her starting point."

"But Joff, that's impossible," protests Dave, "because to move across she would have to move downstream as well."

After forty-two years at our school, it would be tempting to dismiss Joff's story as ramblings brought on by senility. But such a dismissal would be misleading; Joff was not being senile, he was leading into a class that introduced me to Vectors and Parametric Differentiation. For the last three years, Mr. Joffray has brought math alive for me. Whether figuring out the rate of change of the length of my shadow when walking away from the lamppost outside the library, or imagining Joff's beagle being swept into the torrents of a flooded Connecticut River, Joff never fails to animate advanced calculus.

Inspired by Joff's creative teaching, I hounded the director of student tutoring about becoming a math tutor. After several weeks of awaiting a decision, my hopes of becoming a student tutor had waned. One day, seeing only a single, small sheet of paper about the size of a photo in my mailbox, I thought fleetingly of the worst messages inter-school mail could bring, but I hadn't cut any classes, wasn't having academic problems, and didn't think I had cut too many breakfasts. Student tutoring never crossed my mind. Intrigued, for the note's size

ruled out another useless memo about snow days or the new computer network, I twirled in the combination to my mailbox and pulled out the sheet.

"Student Tutoring: Tom Tsing, Algebra II Advanced, Nee Room. Sunday, 4:00." Immediately, I felt a sense of kinship with Tommy. During Freshman year, I too had struggled through Mrs. B's Algebra II Advanced class where her way was *the* way.

Entering the study hall, I knew only the most basic information about Tommy: he was an Asian-born Sophomore who lived in Batch, and this was his first year in the United States. Upon first glance, I saw only the deserted study hall, but in the far corner, hidden almost completely by the odd shadows of the room, a small Asian boy sat stiffly with textbook and notebook aligned neatly in front of him. His textbook seemed to have absorbed his attention; his head was bent over it and even after the door slammed behind me his head never raised. But seeing his expression of bewilderment and his deeply-creased brow, I hurried over to the table.

"Hi. My name is Nat. Are you Tommy?"

He stood quickly, stiffly extended his arm, and haltingly said, "Hello my name is Tommy Tsing. Pleased to meet you," confirming my suspicion that Tommy's problem was twofold: not only did he have trouble with the math, but he also struggled to understand English. That Sunday progressed as every other would: Tommy produced from his neatly-organized binder Mrs. B's immaculate syllabus and I taught the concept-of-the-week. We met again on Tuesday to review homework and on Thursday to prepare for the weekly test.

As the term progressed, much of my enjoyment came because Tommy's face lit up with understanding more frequently, indicating that he was learning. But the learning was not limited to Tommy; I, too, was learning. I learned that what is being taught is not nearly as important as how it is being taught. Unfailingly, whenever I was able to enliven material by making it humorous or by applying it to a real-life situation that could be imagined, Tommy's comprehension skyrocketed. And when Tommy moved from a C at the midterm to a B+ by the end of the trimester, I was proud to have played a part in his success. But perhaps the most gratifying part of tutoring Tommy was that I was able to

emphasize presentation again and again, whether tutoring inner-city Hartford elementary students or learning the second half of Calculus BC largely on my own.

"So what's the topic this week?"

"Vectors and Pro . . ." Tommy stammered.

"Here let me see . . . Oh, Vectors and Projectile Motion . . . say, do you know Mr. Joffray, Tommy?"

"No."

"Well, have you ever seen an old guy, who sort of limps a little, walking his really old dog early in the morning?"

"Yes."

"Now imagine if his dog ran away from him one morning . . . and jumped in the Farmington River . . . and started to swim to the other side."

. . . And Tommy smiled imagining this ridiculous spectacle.

✎   ✎   ✎

WORLD VIEWS AND PERSONAL CONVICTIONS *(8 Essays)*

Essay No. 23

"I'm sorry," said the tree,

"but I have no money.
I have only leaves and apples.
But take my apples . . ."

The Giving Tree, by Shel Silverstein

December 15th. Ms. Lorri Kellogg, founder of the non-profit adoption agency Universal Aid for Children Inc., attended my high school's Human Rights Conference and addressed the deplorable conditions of infants and teenage orphans in war-torn third world countries. She began with a video of Romania which showed children eating from garbage cans, infants in worn-out cloth diapers, and teenagers in their last months of pregnancy. The overwhelming horror of the scenes appalled me. While I sat comfortably, surrounded by classmates who live sheltered lives, there in front of me was the sullen face of a 17-year-old who

looked as if her only savior were death. It broke my heart to discover that, at the dawn of the 21st century, countless orphans were enduring such deprivation and humiliating misfortune. Then, I realized that pity was useless if not followed by action, and I decided to initiate the first high school Universal Aid for Children Reach Out Organization. Subsequent events significantly shaped the essence of who I am today.

The steps necessary to form the organization were challenging; however, with patience and dedication, I prevailed. Ms. Kellogg suggested that I sponsor the country with the most severe problems, and after extensive research I chose El Salvador. Afterwards, I organized a group of thirty-five motivated students and began fundraising efforts and clothing drives. We then wrote letters to the First Lady of El Salvador, hoping to convey our enthusiasm for effecting positive change.

The work involved has been demanding; however, the results and commendations received have been remarkable. After dedicating 600 hours to Reach Out, I was invited by Ms. Kellogg to accompany her to El Salvador to meet the First Lady on October 21st. I am thrilled by this prestigious honor and determined to help the government make reforms within the orphan institutions. In preparation, I recently met with Mrs. Mylene Alvergue, vice-consul of El Salvador in Miami, and expressed the following goals: to furnish the institutions with professional and medical provisions and to enhance the areas of hygiene, education, and health care. Ms. Alvergue agreed and suggested that I inform the First Lady of my intentions.

What do I hope to accomplish by a single visit to a third-world country in the midst of economic despair? What can one small group of high-school students do to institute significant reforms in the face of extreme deprivation? In examining these questions, I believe that information is power. After I assess first-hand the children's most dire needs, I am confident that I will be able to improve their lives. Yes, we are a handful of teenagers facing an enormous challenge; but, we can begin a legacy of hope that will evolve into something greater than all of us. As evidenced in *The Giving Tree*, the desire to give of myself is all I have to offer, but I can rest in the satisfaction of knowing that some day soon lives will be touched in a positive way because I chose not to accept reality.

✎   ✎   ✎

Essay No. 24

I live in a small suburban town, where the atmosphere is slowly being destroyed by the influx of commercial business and development. A great source of anxiety to me is the extent to which this may eradicate the town's heritage and environment . . .

A cool evening breeze wafted over the age-old former municipal court, illuminated by a stately street lamp from the late nineteenth century. Through the rhythmic, dreary swaying of two tall willows, one could perceive the building's simple architecture: four perpendicular walls and a sharply pitched roof. Windows were few and unadorned. The single magnificent feature of the court was a towering steeple, evidence of its early service as a Protestant church. Once, children and their parents gathered there in their best attire for Sunday sermons. Now, the ancient edifice stood silent, a lifeless presence dwarfed by the vastness of the cloudy sky. As the clouds drifted, a glimmer of moonlight fell on the building, lighting the hallway within. The corridor was enveloped in white, from the porcelain tiles to the alabaster walls. Two antique benches, crafted from mahogany, stood at either end of the hall, their splendor obscured by a thick layer of dust.

A few minutes later, the main door creaked open, and the street lamp projected onto the hallway the silhouette of a lone, plain-looking man. He moved confidently through the courthouse, since after his duty in the army he had served as magistrate within these walls. Moving toward one of the four inner doors, he thrust it open with flamboyance, admiring his former office with the strength of a thousand memories. Thoughtfully, he continued to his chair and sat down. Taking up the gavel, he smiled; the furnishings in the room had neither been replaced nor refurbished since its construction, and they remained as solid as the day they had been made. Poised upon his former judicial post, he relived his favorite cases. Most were neighborly quarrels or property disputes, and none were as brutal as those he was hearing about these days. Disturbed by these thoughts, the man arose and moved toward the door once more, and after swiftly passing through the corridor, he left the building. As he exited, he felt something bound over his foot. Since winter was approaching, he believed it was probably a squirrel hoarding

food; reaching into his coat pocket, he produced a half-eaten sandwich, bent down, and placed it on the clayish ground for the animal, should it return.

An hour later, a black, polished oxford crushed that sandwich, and the brilliant glow of a lantern flooded the small courthouse. The man who loomed in the doorway was nattily dressed: the suit he sported was expertly tailored, his overcoat was of the finest wool, and his elegant hat was tilted back at a dashing angle. He was young, no more than thirty years of age, and he walked quickly through the hall, glancing around furtively and taking deep breaths from a smoldering menthol. Lackadaisically sliding into a bench, he stirred up the age-old dust, which rose quickly around him. Irritated, he continued to move about, scrutinizing the rooms. The furnishings, he thought, would bring quite a sum through auction, as would the oil paintings on the walls—portraits of men who had contributed to the community. Then he could bring in a blasting crew to level the building. He found the court's history to be of passing interest but was deeply attracted to the profitability of building a shopping center on the land.

Content with his plans, he pictured himself a dozen times richer and smiled approvingly to himself. As he turned to depart, he noticed a half-destroyed window and decided to end its misery. With a swift and brutal kick, he shattered the remaining glass, rending a spider's web in the process. Approaching the door, he turned off the switch that gave power to the street lamp; no sense in wasting electricity and, therefore, money. He casually dropped his cigarette on the tiled floor and stamped it out with his heel. Heading for his car, he murmured to himself that the trees would have to be cut down to extend the parking lot. That would cost a fair amount, but he hoped that selling the lumber would pay for most of it. Getting into his sedan, he looked around and wondered why people had lobbied against his venture; after all, it could only bring the town revenue. Then there was the roar of a Buick six-cylinder, and as its drone dissipated into nothingness, silence descended upon the courthouse once again, to remain until the demolition crew arrived the following morning.

✎   ✎   ✎

Essay No. 25

[This essay was accompanied by a photograph of a saddle shoe taken by the applicant during a trip to Poland.]

I wore saddle shoes five days a week for nine years of my life. I started Kindergarten with the clunky leather ones that were most common and did not think much about them. In the third grade I had grown to hate my uniform and, like all my friends, tried to find the lightest, most un-saddle-shoe-like saddle shoe. I wore what I could find, plastic blue and white imitations, until the sixth grade. Then it became popular to wear the old style, clunky, black heavy, hard leather again. In the eighth grade my classmates and I signed our good-byes on our shoes, and I wore my saddle shoes home from the last day of grammar school with a heavy heart. Now I wear those saddle shoes as a fashion statement, but they serve more as a gentle reminder of old school friends the years have left behind.

The shoe in this picture is not mine. When I took this shot, however, it certainly felt like it belonged to me. During the spring of my sophomore year, I spent a week in Poland visiting concentration camps followed by a week of sight-seeing in Israel. I was accompanied by seven-thousand Jewish students, Rabbis, teachers, and Holocaust survivors from all over the world. Together we made up "The March of the Living," an annual program run by the Bureau of Jewish Education in which students from around the world meet in Poland and Israel to witness Holocaust Remembrance Day and Israeli Independence Day.

On my final day in Poland I entered the gates of Majdonek concentration camp, only a few hours away from the village where my grandparents had lived. I took this picture there, at the back of an old barrack that has been converted into a museum. I thought of my family then; my heritage and beliefs. I realized that for nine years a shoe had identified who I was, and now I was barefoot. I was only what my past had made me, and over fifty years ago another girl had a similar definition. This tie came not just because of our shoes, but because of our religion and our love for it.

Years ago a girl wore that saddle shoe to school. She marveled at its heavy weight and saw her friends walking in matching pairs. Unfortunately, looking at the bright white leather amid the faded brown

of loafers, heels, and lace-ups, I knew that girl's fate all too well. They had taken those shoes from her. They had taken her. And I was thankful to have my own pair waiting in my closet across the world; thankful for my family, their love, and our tradition.

✎   ✎   ✎

Essay No. 26

In the Spring of my freshman year I was invited to travel to Albany, New York, to lobby for increased school aid for the New York state budget. While this was a memorable experience, it was what happened on the bus ride home that affected the rest of my high-school years.

The bus was filled with about thirty passengers. A diverse mixture of students, teachers, parents, and administrators. Somehow the conversation turned to the lack of AIDS education in the health curriculum. The talk led to the formation of a committee. The South Huntington School District AIDS Committee was born with twelve members. Of the four student members I was the only freshman.

The Committee visited schools, heard speakers, and discussed frightening statistics about the deadly disease of AIDS. The universal reaction was: "How could this disease affect a small suburban community like ours?" We came to the realization that AIDS could affect anyone, anywhere, anytime. Should we write to the state education department and request a review of the curriculum? Maybe we could just have a lecturer come to the school. After much deliberation we decided to implement an AIDS Peer Education Program. Our goal: for our high-school students "teach" our junior-high students. That summer we gathered forty sophomores, juniors, and seniors to "train." For five days we went through rigorous training. We learned all about AIDS, teen pregnancy, STD's, and condom use. We also learned how to present the material in an orderly manner.

School began and we continued our training during weekly evening meetings. It was in February that the true test began. Each pair of "peer educators" was assigned to a seventh-grade health class. At first it was difficult. Each time my partner or I said "vaginal secretion" the class would break into laughter. [We broke into laughter too the first three or

four times . . . okay, maybe eight or nine times.] Toward the last two lessons it seemed like some of what we were saying was actually sinking in. I was having a great time while teaching these kids. In one role-playing exercise I played a guy who was trying to get his girlfriend to have sex with him. My partner played the girlfriend. Every pair of eyes was glued to our acting, not because it was Oscar caliber, but because the kids associated with the situation.

The program was a great success that year and an even greater success the next year when the district granted permission to extend the program to include ninth-grade science classes. By this time, I was the only student left on the AIDS Committee. All the other students had graduated, and I took on an even greater role in the program. When we visited PTA meetings and Board of Education meetings, I spoke for the group. I represented our AIDS group as a member of the 1995 Teen Health Conference Planning Board. When we won an award for having one of the best AIDS programs in our county, I accepted it on behalf of our school.

The AIDS program took on a special meaning to me. As we enter the third year of the program, I'm the only student who has been there from the start. Throughout my four years of high school, I have devoted many hours to the success of our program. I am proud of my work, and I am even prouder of the fact that our program is saving lives.

✎   ✎   ✎

Essay No. 27

I have often wondered whether the United States has an obligation to get involved in the internal conflicts of other countries. When does the power to intervene become an obligation to act? I gained some insight into this dilemma when a small part of the Bosnian war spilled into my home last year.

During the height of the Bosnian conflict, my family was informed that twenty Bosnian students were airlifted out of the mountains surrounding Sarajevo. A relief organization called "Bridge for Humanity" sought families in the United States that would take in these

Muslim teenagers for the school year. The need was urgent because the U.S. government would not let them board planes until homes had been found.

My parents and I spent at least a week contemplating whether we should offer. At first I resisted, fearing the obligations that I would be forced to undertake. I knew it would be my job to help this visitor integrate with the students at our school and to look out for him in social situations. Eventually, my parents agreed, but they left the final decision to me. The deciding factor was my parents' reminder of the six-million people who were killed in World War II. Many of these Jews, gypsies, and other "undesirables" had tried to flee Germany and Eastern Europe, but found no country that would accept them. Being Jewish, I found it easy to imagine how desperate I would have been in the same situation, needing someone to rescue me. The choice was made.

Emir arrived last October with one small bag. He told us that he had crawled out of Sarajevo through a narrow tunnel leading to the mountains beyond the city. He crawled for many hours in this hot confined space, terrified of being caught and shot by the Serbs. I doubt that Emir looked back during this journey. The building where he had once lived had been blown up months before. He survived in cellars, with little food, and electricity for only five hours each week. Behind Emir, the bombs fell on his city every day.

When Emir arrived at my house, for the first day he could not stop smiling. He appeared jovial and appreciative of the United States and of my family. Soon, however, it became clear that Emir had not escaped Bosnia completely. His inner rage began to emerge. His hatred of the Serbs permeated his thoughts and judgments. Eventually, he began to hate the United States too. To Emir, America's failure to prevent Serbian atrocities made it evil. He found it reprehensible that some Americans opposed sending troops to defend the Bosnian minorities. He hated Americans that would not risk their lives to save his people.

The six months that Emir lived in my home are the most difficult that I can remember. Many nights I would stay up very late talking to him about his negative attitude toward the United States. As he attacked our society, I found myself becoming defensive, then angry. When my mother found butcher knives hidden in his drawers, anger turned to fear.

I began to understand the depth of the trauma Emir had experienced in Bosnia, even as I pulled away from him. I discovered some limits to what I could give.

It is now six months later. I have learned that the casualties of war cannot be measured merely by life and death. Those who survive may live with pain, and those who try to help may feel its repercussions. This experience brought a new dimension to my life, as well as a new appreciation of my advantages in the United States. As we are a privileged nation, I feel we have an obligation to aid both oppressed and impoverished countries. There are risks, there are rewards, and there are degrees of failure. Sometimes those we help may hate us for being less than they imagined. But because we did not look away when we were needed and had something to give, we have lived up to our moral obligation.

✎   ✎   ✎

Essay No. 28

I close my eyes and can still hear her—the little girl with a voice so strong and powerful we could hear her halfway down the block. She was a Russian peasant who asked for money and in return gave the only thing she had—her voice. I paused outside a small shop and listened. She brought to my mind the image of Little Orphan Annie. I could not understand the words she sang, but her voice begged for attention. It stood out from the noises of Arbat Street, pure and impressive, like the chime of a bell. She sang from underneath an old-style lamp post in the shadow of a building, her arms extended and head thrown back. She was small and of unremarkable looks. Her brown hair escaped the bun it had been pulled into, and she occasionally reached up to remove a stray piece from her face. Her clothing I can't recall. Her voice, on the other hand, is permanently imprinted on my mind.

I asked one of the translators about the girl. Elaina told me that she and hundreds of others like her throughout the former Soviet Union add to their families' income by working on the streets. The children are unable to attend school, and their parents work fulltime. These children know that the consequence of an unsuccessful day is no food for the

table. Similar situations occurred during the Depression in the United States, but those American children were faceless shoeshine boys of the twenties. This girl was real to me.

When we walked past her I gave her money. It was not out of pity but rather admiration. Her smile of thanks did not interrupt her singing. The girl watched us as we walked down the street. I know this because when I looked back she smiled again. We shared that smile, and I knew I would never forget her courage and inner strength. She was only a child, yet was able to pull her own weight during these uncertain times. On the streets of Moscow, she used her voice to help her family survive. For this "Annie," there is no Daddy Warbucks to come to the rescue. Her salvation will only come when Russia and its people find prosperity.

✎   ✎   ✎

Essay No. 29

On April 15, 1947, a man strode out to first base at Ebbets Field in Brooklyn, a black man wearing Dodger blue. This was Jackie Robinson, a significant figure for a number of reasons, but the one that made him so special was his absolute inequality. The inequity of his position in the arena of race set him apart, and his superior abilities as a ball player placed him a rung above his contemporaries. That is the essence of rewarding performance—to raise one person above the pack, to place him in a more esteemed position so that we can all learn from him, learn to emulate him, and learn to pull ourselves out of the quagmire of mediocrity and reach his height.

Growth and evolution proceed in a stepwise fashion, and while equality is obviously the loftiest goal toward which we can strive, transforming individuals into role models is how we better ourselves. Otherwise, we muddle along in our brief existence, not having exacted any change, not having accomplished anything.

Not everyone can be singled out, however, for if we all have our own particular agendas without any form of unity, then our society cannot progress together. What we must do, then, is to balance individual achievement with the needs of the group and identify barriers that separate us as a people so that we can break them down. We can be equal

and excellent at the same time, insofar as we are equal in our goal to emulate the accomplishments of an individual role model. In Jackie Robinson's time, America was practically united in its aversion to integration. He became an icon, and this country took a hard look at itself. Sometimes a little inequality helps.

Essay No. 30

I had a mental image of them standing there, wearing ragged clothes, hot and depressed, looking upon us as intruders in their world. They would sneer at our audacity. We would invade their territory only to take pictures and observe them like tourists.

We climbed out of the van and faced eleven men assembled in the shade. My mental image was confirmed. My class, consisting of twelve primarily white, middle-class students, felt out of place. Our Politics of Food curriculum at Governor's School, a summer environmental program, included an interview with migrant workers. We were at a farm worker labor camp in southern New Jersey, but judging from the rural landscape, it may as well have been Iowa. I felt like a trespasser.

So we were surprised when one man—the oldest of the group—approached and offered each of us a piece of candy. The man appeared remarkably coarse; his beige skin was leathery like a crocodile's, and yellow teeth jutted from his gum line. His shoddy turquoise tee-shirt and blue jeans conveyed a sense of basic humanity. His broken English was barely discernible. Fortunately, a man wearing a nearly clean denim shirt and jeans stepped forward to interpret.

Contrary to my preconceptions, the men seemed glad to see us. They bantered and joked like office staff on a coffee break. They told of their isolation and the rarity of meeting other people, let alone students. They seemed genuinely interested in helping our study. Just as we asked about their backgrounds, they questioned us about ours. "Do any of you have jobs?" asked one worker.

The old man told us his story as we all walked around the fields. He was sixty-eight, had immigrated from Colombia at a young age, and had been working at this labor camp for almost twenty years. Long since

divorced, he had been performing unskilled labor all his life. The younger workers conveyed similar stories. They generally had a high-school education and moved to the United States for financial reasons. I was surprised that one man in his twenties had a girlfriend in New York, drove a taxi half the year, and hoped to attend college soon. Their lives put our teen anxiety in perspective. Sure, we may become upset when the car is taken away for the weekend. We may be preoccupied with wearing the right clothes. Yet these men had nowhere to go on Saturday nights. They wore dirty, shabby attire. And it did not matter.

Before we left, the old man picked twelve small cucumbers and proudly gave them to the class. I had never enjoyed eating cucumbers before. But since then I have become quite fond of them.

✎　　✎　　✎

LESSONS LEARNED, SETBACKS AND SUCCESSES *(6 Essays)*

Essay No. 31

I walked into the first class that I have ever taught and confronted utter chaos. The four students in my Latin class were engaged in a heated spitball battle. They were all following the lead of Andrew, a tall eleven-year-old African-American boy.

Andrew turned to me and said, "Why are we learning Latin if no one speaks it? This a waste of time."

I broke out in a cold sweat. I thought, "How on Earth am I going to teach this kid?"

It was my first day of Summerbridge, a nationwide collaborative of thirty-six public and private high schools. Its goal is to foster a desire to learn in young, underprivileged students, while also exposing college and high-school students to teaching. Since I enjoy tutoring, I decided to apply to the program. I thought to myself, "Teaching can't be that difficult. I can handle it." I have never been more wrong in my life.

After what seemed like an eternity, I ended that first class feeling as though I had accomplished nothing. Somehow I needed to catch

Andrew's attention. For the next two weeks, I tried everything from indoor chariot races to a Roman toga party, but nothing seemed to work.

During the third week, after I had exhausted all of my ideas, I resorted to a game that my Latin teacher had used. A leader yells out commands in Latin and the students act out the commands. When I asked Andrew to be the leader, I found the miracle that I had been seeking. He thought it was great that he could order the teacher around with commands such as "jump in place" and "touch the window." I told him that if he asked me in Latin to do something, I would do it as long as he would do the same. With this agreement, I could teach him new words outside the classroom, and he could make his teacher hop on one foot in front of his friends. Andrew eventually gained a firm grasp of Latin.

Family night occurred during the last week of Summerbridge. We explained to the parents what we had accomplished. At the conclusion, Andrew's mom thanked me for teaching him Latin. She said, "Andrew wanted to speak Latin with someone, so he taught his younger brother."

My mouth fell open. I tempered my immediate desire to utter, "Andrew did what?" I was silent for a few seconds as I tried to regain my composure, but when I responded, I was unable to hide my surprise.

That night I remembered a comment an English teacher had made to me. I had asked her, "Why did you become a teacher?"

She responded with a statement that perplexed me at the time. She said, "There is nothing greater than empowering someone with the love of knowledge." Now, I finally understood what she meant.

When I returned to Summerbridge for my second summer, the first words out of Andrew's mouth were, "Is there going to be a Latin class this year?"

✏   ✏   ✏

Essay No. 32

This much I remember: my mother walking into my room and saying the six words which changed my views of people and my own actions forever—"You made him cry, you know." Brief moments of that day rise and fall in my memory, with certain portions crystal clear and other parts shrouded in mystery. Yet no matter how much of the story I can

accurately recall, I will never forget this one phrase. But to avoid getting ahead of myself, I should start at the beginning.

I was rocking back and forth on the swingset behind my house next to Mark Kramer. Mark had always been bigger than I. He had also, for as long as I could remember, been my friend. From those earliest pre-school days at The Training Depot, we were inseparable. I don't recall how or why we became fast friends, but I do know that some of my earliest and fondest memories come from the days I spent with him.

It was not for Mark's size that I respected him most, but more for all of the qualities that he possessed which I lacked. He was braver than I ever thought I could be and more comfortable talking to people, especially girls. His sense of humor never failed him, and he always managed to make everyone laugh. Yet, although he made many friends over the years I knew him, he never deserted me. This is why it hurt me so much the day my mom told me the outcome of my actions.

We were well into one of our insult wars which we waged whenever our parents were out of the room. We never took it seriously, at least not until that day. We were both very quick thinkers, and to us the "war" had been simply a warped means of recreation. But on this day, Mark dug out the heavy artillery—an insult book. As a result, I was forced beyond the old standbys into more original forms of cut-downs. No "your mother" cracks would hold up against him today. No, I was in for a fight, and shortly after we began, I realized I was losing. I admit that I began to panic, and I was reaching for something, anything, which would act as a final, crushing blow. In a daze, I blurted out, "Oh yeah?! Well you stutter!"

I did not think much about the comment at the time. For one thing, it made me the clear victor. That one phrase shut him up for good. Sure it was mean, attacking him in the one weak spot which we both knew he had but never spoke of. We were playing around, or so I thought. Mark soon left to go home, uneventfully, and in defeat. I did not think that I would ever hear of it again and had put it completely out of mind until my mother came into my room later that night to tell me what I had done.

Five words . . . and realization. Suddenly, a shocking image appeared in my mind. I envisioned this boy, my first true friend and the first person outside of my family that I respected, hunched over and weeping. This brief moment, which I had brushed off as nothing, affected Mark profoundly, and I had not even realized it. I claimed to be

Mark's friend, but I had been blind to the pain which he experienced as a result of his minor speech impediment. To me, the comment had been a joke, but to him it had been an insult harsher than any other. And it had cut this brave, imposing boy more than I could have imagined.

Of course I apologized immediately and I told him that I had not known what the impact of my actions would be. And, as is often the case with childhood friendships, all was soon forgiven. However, at least as far as I was concerned, all was not forgotten. Although Mark eventually stopped stuttering and later moved to Cleveland, I have often replayed that moment in my mind. For me, it serves as a reminder of the terrible power that I can have over another person's feelings and of the need for analyzing my words before I speak.

But finally, and most importantly, this moment showed me what it was to needlessly hurt another human being. I realized that as easy as it is to make someone feel awful, it is just as easy to make him or her feel terrific. Since that time, I have made an effort to spare people from experiencing pointless pain from my words and actions. Mark Kramer probably does not remember the day I made him cry. But I have never been able to forget it: the flippant attitude I had when I told him of his flaw, the shock I felt when I learned of the result, and the decision I made to see that it would never happen again.

✎   ✎   ✎

Essay No. 33

Ten years from now Tim Dickson won't even remember my name. The unknowing recipient of my undying love for two years, Tim had been everything a girl could ever ask for: smart, handsome, witty, athletic, with a voice that could make angels weep. Everyone knew his name. To a shy little country mouse, nearly invisible in our student body, he was the epitome of manliness. I sat in my corner of room C-119 and gazed adoringly at his profile as he amazed the class of Modern World History with his dashing style. Carefully planning the routes to my classes to coincide with his, I was his silent shadow.

After fourteen months, contrary to my hopes, Tim still was not aware of my existence. Determined to bring myself to his attention, I staged my entrance to his heart with all the flair I could muster. I would

breach his defenses at the next history oral presentation in the guise of the dashing Cardinal Richelieu.

It was now or never! Striding into the classroom, my head raised, eyes flashing, I stood proudly, the colors of my eighteenth-century costume catching the light and giving me courage. My opening line shook with tight emotion. "Gentlemen, I am disgusted!" My voice alternately lashed out in rage and purred in soft persuasion. I gloried in my elocution. Each word was power. My voice rose to a brilliant conclusion, and I stood with my arms outstretched and my head bowed in submission.

Dead silence.

My left knee trembled uncontrollably. Why did no one speak? My hands began to shake so I pulled them behind me—like one condemned. My eyes gauged the distance to the door.

Then someone began to clap. More joined in. Tim looked into my eyes—and smiled. He smiled!

Joy, oh joy. My soul overflowed with rapture. I had done it! He noticed me! All the shame, all the worry, and all the castagation melted away in that moment. I knew how to make him love me. I simply had to speak better, sing better, act better, and write better than anyone else.

Determined, I joined competitions, played in concerts, and wrote essays that were read in class. When Tim transferred to the A.P. class, so did I. I threw myself into class discussions, attempting to dazzle him with my intelligence and intrepidity. Making friends with his friends, I dogged his steps.

The next summer Tim moved away. I never heard from him again. But the transformation in me had taken place. Now I was involved for the simple pleasure of being involved. Challenging people surrounded me. Biff taught me to love. Dave taught me to laugh. Ramez taught me to break my limits. Alit gave me confidence. Whenever I was in danger of reverting to a wallflower, one of my new friends would drag me into another club or activity.

In every foray into the threatening world of "school activities," I still feel an overpowering impulse to run. But although my feelings haven't changed, my actions have. My stomach still tightens when I enter a room of unfamiliar faces, but I walk in. I still want to run from risk and recrimination, but I keep my feet firmly planted.

Tim Dickson was the single best thing that ever happened to me, all because he didn't know me from Adam.

✐   ✐   ✐

Essay No. 34

I want to learn to take risks. I want to change my attitude about taking chances. Assessing my academic and extracurricular achievements, I am proud of my accomplishments. I see myself as an open-minded, goal-oriented person who achieves and succeeds through hard work and determination. How much of that success is a result of staying on comfortable ground?

I began wondering about the range of my abilities when I attended Northwestern University's Theater Arts Program last summer. The theme of the institute, announced by the director, was: "Dare to fail gloriously." This idea encouraged participants to take bold risks on the stage. Over time I applied this philosophy to my acting and my life. I began the Northwestern program as a quasi-accomplished actress with a hunger to absorb all I could about acting. I emerged not only a well-rounded thespian, but also a more secure person with a new outlook. I knew that there was something about my life that I wanted to change and could change. Now, as I approach college, I am committed to continuing successes and occasional glorious failures.

The first day at Northwestern I was asked to choose among three subjects in technical theater, ranking them in order of preference. Set Design was my first choice, followed by Costumes, and finally Stage Lighting. Much to my dismay, I was assigned to the lighting crew. Though disappointed, I tried to stay open-minded. I knew nothing about lighting, but followed the slogan which kept repeating in my head: "Dare to fail. . . ."

By the third lighting session, I had discovered a new passion: I was eager to learn everything I could about lights. Having always been a performer who enjoyed the limelight, I had never realized the skill required to create it properly. In my free time I climbed the catwalks, memorized cues, circuited lamps, or changed gels. My competence was recognized when I was selected head light board operator for the final production of the summer.

If the choice to study lighting had not been made for me, I would have missed an enriching opportunity. The experience taught me to take

more risks, rather than to follow the most certain path to success. The exposure made me realize how limited my perspective had been in approaching new situations. The choice that was made for me, undesirable as it seemed at the outset, taught me to embrace new experiences and ideas.

I believe that "the past is prologue." In college I will take more risks, convinced that the potential rewards outweigh my fear of failure. I have stopped trying to select a major, and am committed to studying in many academic disciplines before deciding on a field of concentration.

Accepting the possibility of failure is a new concept for me. While I have had recognition for academics, performing arts, community service, and athletic achievements, perhaps I have missed some enriching experiences because my certainty of success was doubtful. I will not avoid such opportunities in the future since I am changing my philosophy of life: I am learning to take risks.

✎   ✎   ✎

Essay No. 35

For many years, I have had difficulty concentrating on my schoolwork. Although my parents provided me with a private-school education and with tutors, I still didn't achieve the grades that I desired even though I was highly motivated. Therefore, I welcomed my parents' invitation to visit a doctor who could evaluate me to see if there was a physical basis for my difficulties. When I was finally diagnosed with Attention Deficit Disorder (ADD), I had mixed emotions. At first, I was relieved that the condition had been identified and that I could obtain treatment and learn to overcome this handicap. However, I was not pleased to have a condition that interfered with my learning. The challenge of learning to live with and conquer ADD provides me with daily insights into myself.

Before I realized there was a possibility that I had a learning disability, I was very insecure about my intelligence level. I couldn't grasp concepts that were taught in class, so I often gave up and allowed myself to daydream. I would study for tests and take notes, yet when I got my scores back, they weren't what I expected. I felt incapable of ever doing well, no matter how hard I tried. I came to the conclusion that this problem was not my fault, and I didn't know how to deal with it.

When the doctor told me I had ADD and he could prescribe medications to help, I was upset. Whenever I had heard of others who had ADD, I had always regarded them negatively. I had the impression that they were people who were never going to amount to anything because they were limited in ability. Even though my doctor informed me that this wasn't true, I still felt embarrassed. I planned not to tell anyone, not even my sisters. Furthermore, I was worried that I might have to be on medication for the rest of my life.

After a series of discussions with my parents and my doctor, I had the choice of using the medicine Ritalin or dealing with problem on my own. My doctor explained that the medicine was not a crutch, but an aid. It wasn't going to make me smarter or force me to concentrate involuntarily; I still had to make a conscious effort to focus on my work. Since I had been dealing with my unknown problem by myself, I decided to try the Ritalin. The only people who knew were my parents and my tutor, and I planned to keep it that way.

It has been six months since I was diagnosed with ADD, and my views have changed drastically. My theory that everyone with ADD is ignorant has been proven wrong. My doctor informed me that more people than I thought had ADD, and some are even adults with prestigious jobs. He also said that I should never be insecure about my intelligence. It was as if I had been doing my work with one hand tied behind my back; now with a little aid, my hands were untied! Most important, I am improving in my schoolwork and maintaining a better relationship with my friends.

Once I realized that dealing with my learning problem was helping my life, I no longer had a problem. I understand that I shouldn't be ashamed of something that can't be helped. I have enough self-confidence to know that it is all right to be different. Indeed, I have learned an important lesson about self-perception: It's not what we think of ourselves; rather, it's what we *make* of ourselves that matters.

✎　　✎　　✎

Essay No. 36

"They look alike, they walk alike, at times they even talk alike." That's the theme from the old *Patty Duke Show* and was, I thought, the theme

for the people of Lafayette, California. I moved from Oakland to Lafayette when I was in the seventh grade, and I found that I was doing more than moving over the hill. I was moving from a city brimming with diversity to a place where everyone seemed ominously similar. At age twelve I was facing the challenge of how and whether to fit in.

Every day was a struggle for me. Being new at a school was trying enough, but attempting to be an individual at a new school was virtually inconceivable. I tried to be bizarre to gain attention and win friends, but I ended up the subject of everyone's extended index finger and of countless whispers and laughs. A few people sympathized with me and did their best to help me. To them I was and still am grateful. Others, however, did their best to ridicule me. These people had a lasting effect on my life that, eventually, would aid me.

In high school I discovered an important outlet that would reshape my attitude and my mind—drama. I enrolled in Drama 1 the first year I was eligible to do so, and I became president of the Drama Club. I somehow got the lead in the school play, Thornton Wilder's *Our Town*. I also appeared in a small theater company's production of *Guys and Dolls*. Performing brought me great pleasure and enhanced my growing confidence. The next year I landed the lead in the school play again and participated in two plays at a community theater. I entered the improvisation competition at the college and won, shocking myself. I had gained an identity. I was an actor.

When I step on stage, the first minute is agony. My throat is dry. My breathing is unsteady and sweat drips down my back. I am terrified. I love it. To me, it doesn't matter if a play is great. Just the thrill of getting up on stage as another person is incredible. When I perform in front of a crowd, I want to make the audience care. I want to exhaust them with my passion so that they leave discussing the play. I want to help the players on stage with me to be better actors. I want to be an actor whose characters seem so real that they cause discomfort or insight, joy or sadness.

I found myself using life experience as a major contributor to my drama. The people I hated for their teasing at intermediate school became very valuable. When I need to dislike someone or something in a role, I bring all those people to mind. When I need to feel grateful to someone, I think of the choice few who wanted to help me. Emotions are easy to evoke with the proper stimuli.

Although the move to the land of clones at age twelve seemed like a personal hell at first, perhaps it was for the best. If I had not been surrounded by what I perceived as anonymity, I might not have found out who I really was. Now I have the opportunity to become anyone. Acting has given me a chance to become whomever I please. What more could I want? Mom, Dad, the move seemed like a questionable idea, but thank you for forcing it upon me. It turned out to be the opportunity of my lifetime.

✎   ✎   ✎

PREOCCUPATIONS AND PASSIONS
(7 Essays)

Essay No. 37

I am an addict. I tell people I could stop anytime, but deep inside, I know I am lying. I need to listen to music, to write music, to play music every day. I can't go a whole day without, at the very least, humming or whistling the tunes that crowd my head. I sing myself hoarse each morning in the shower, and playing the trumpet leaves a red mouthpiece-shaped badge of courage on my lips all day. I suspect that if someone were to look at my blood under a microscope, they would see, between the platelets and t-cells, little black musical notes coursing through my body.

On many occasions I've woken my family (and perhaps the neighborhood) composing on the piano early in the morning. Other times, my mother will admonish, "It's too late to play the trumpet." But I can't understand why people wouldn't want to hear music any time of the day. Keeping the music bottled up is more than I can bear. "I never worry about you sneaking up on me," my friend once admitted to me. "I've never seen you walking without humming or whistling to yourself."

For me, playing the trumpet is the opiate of music in its purest form. I love to play in all types of ensembles. I'm not just addicted to one kind of music; I couldn't imagine limiting myself like that. Choosing just one kind of music would be worse than choosing one food to eat for the rest of my life. Playing orchestral music, for example, I become a

sharpshooter. Waiting, I hide behind rows of string players, ready to jump out with a staccato attack that pierces the hearts of the audience. Playing in an orchestra, I can be Atlas, holding the other musicians above my head, or Icarus, flying through a solo in a desperate attempt to reach the heavens.

Completely different, small jazz ensembles are like a conversation with your closest friends. "So," someone asks, "what do you think about. . . ." We mull it over together, and then each has a say. I build on what the piano proclaimed, or disagree with the saxophone. Playing jazz like this makes me giddy; jazz musicians know that music isn't little dots on a piece of paper, but a feeling that makes you want to stomp your feet, shout for joy, or grab a partner and swing. Taking a solo, I extend my wings, a baby bird jumping out of my nest for the first time. Flapping madly, I hope that by some act of seeming magic my music will fly on its own.

Not only am I an addict, I am also a pusher. The schools in the neighboring community are unable to afford musical instruction, so each week several other high school musicians and I teach music at an elementary school on the east side of town. I work with all of the trumpets for an hour before we join the other instruments to play as a band. Having tutored since freshman year, I've seen my students gradually improve. Four years ago, few of them could read music.

This year, one of my best students won a scholarship to the Stanford Jazz Workshop. Many students from the east side of town never continue on through high school. At our last homecoming game, all of my students came and played with the pep band. One student, who had been struggling in school, confided in me that playing with us had made him excited about attending high school for the first time. That afternoon, I saw a new music addiction forming; it was almost better than being hooked myself.

✎   ✎   ✎

Essay No. 38

My second home doesn't actually exist, tangibly. It's a hidden corner on the vast electronic world of the information superhighway: America Online's Simulation City.

I've always preferred the world of fantasy to that of reality. It's why I write, and why I act, and why I've been nicknamed "bookworm" more times than I can count. So when I saw the notice last January about a new weekly role-playing game forming on-line, it was only natural for me to check it out. I'd never role-played before, not so much as a round of Dungeons & Dragons, and I was curious. When I "stepped" into the chatroom that first Thursday night ten months ago, I had no idea what to expect. What I found was a community of bright, imaginative people who, like me, never quite fit into the real world.

There's Sandra, a newlywed who keeps us updated on the "joys of matrimony" and the antics of her husband—like the new color he created when he threw all her clothes into the washer at once. We all nearly died of jealously the night she missed the "sim" because Tom surprised her with tickets to *Phantom of the Opera*.

There's Mariann, a graduate English student at the University of Maryland, the group's academic and token conservative. It was her idea to start a weekly sim newsletter. She's helped me out on more than one English paper ("Mariann! Emergency! How much do you know about the Allegory of the Cave in Plato's *Republic*?"), and amuses us all with her passionate support of the Republican Revolution.

There's West, an unabashed lady's man. He's probably the first person to receive an official warning from AOL for sexual harassment within the context of a role-playing game. He can drive us nuts, but Sim City wouldn't be the same without him. And there's Danica, my 3,000-miles-away twin. We started talking via e-mail when we realized we were taking the SAT the same day—and were amazed when we received identical scores. Our fast and furious conversation hasn't stopped since. Our similarities are uncanny: we've taken the same courses in school, been in many of the same plays, read the same books (no one else has ever understood my *Schrodinger's Cat* references!), agreed with the same philosophies, and laughed at the same jokes. We've co-written stories together, and our styles are indistinguishable. Two weeks ago, we finally met face to face when her dad came to D.C. for a conference and brought her along. We met up at Planet Hollywood in a mystery-novel-like scene: I stood outside in a black skirt with a braid over my shoulder, watching for a girl with short brown hair and a silver

pentacle necklace. She slept over at my house, I played tour guide the next day, and we talked for 26 straight hours.

There's also Michael, Sue, Vic, Manda, Ruth, Jon, and a half dozen others who have become my extended family in the last year. Oh, I've heard the warnings about the Internet: you can't take anyone at face value; it's full of socially maladjusted kooks; the sense of community it creates is false; it'll ultimately drive people farther apart. I've read *Silicon Snake Oil* and listened on C-SPAN to Senator Exxon's diatribes about the evils of the information superhighway. But I've seen its virtues. I'm part of a generation growing up with this new communication medium, and I've found a place where I fit in among the thirty-seven million Internet users.

The America Online Thursday Sim Group is a community in every sense of the word. We met because of a common interest in creating a simulated world we can live in for a few hours a week, and have grown over the months to care about the people behind the characters. We remember birthdays, cheer each other up on bad days, celebrate accomplishments, and are there to just talk to, about everything from Jello to the afterlife. Like any family, we've had our spats (like the time when Mariann refused to run a story about Danica's character coming out of the closet, because it contradicted her idea of what values the sim should encourage), but we've been strong enough to overcome them. And if it weren't for our hidden corner, my 3,000-miles-away twin and I would never have met.

✎   ✎   ✎

Essay No. 39

As a young boy, my father often took me to Wrigley Field. I was so intrigued by the sounds of the crowd mixed with the scent of hot dogs and peanuts in the air. The ivy clinging to the outfield walls contained memories of past seasons and the Cubs' losing tradition. As I analyze my attachment to this venerated shrine to baseball, I realize that my summer days working there helped me to mature, and taught me some sobering lessons. Other summer days relaxing in the bleachers suited my personality well.

In April of 1994, I began my summer job with the opening of the baseball season. During weekend games, I pushed a dessert cart from skybox to skybox, with the assignment to sell as many desserts as possible. It was fortunate that the success of the enterprise did not depend on my sales. Being somewhat shy with strangers, at first I had difficulty looking my customers in the eye. I stared down at the ground and mumbled the dessert choices. I am sure there was a universal feeling among the skybox guests that they were going deaf, as they always asked me to speak louder. The other employee assigned to the dessert cart always seemed to have more "tips" at the end of the day. That was when my sense of competition and pride took over. First I risked looking up; then I stopped mumbling; then I spoke louder; and to my surprise, I even started to have a confident personality with strangers. I was growing up, and I was proud of myself.

People all over the United States will remember the summer of 1994 as the summer of the baseball strike. I will remember it as the summer I got "laid off." I had always wanted to work at Wrigley Field, and was so proud of my new success. I was one happy fifteen-year old. By August, I had half my earnings saved for a new Kurzweil keyboard.

The tension was mounting as the playoffs and World Series approached. Another tension was also accelerating between the owners and the players, but I did not take it seriously. Then it happened. Suddenly, the scent of hot dogs was gone, and there was no one to see the ivy in full bloom. The players and owners had forgotten the perfection and beauty of the game. It was shocking to realize that my heroes caused me to lose my job; the millions of dollars they were making were not enough. I could not believe that my dream of a new keyboard was gone. This suddenly seemed insignificant when Javier, one of my co-workers, expressed his anxiety about feeding his family of five. I wondered how many other families would seriously suffer financially when their paychecks stopped arriving. The word "strike" in baseball now had a sobering new meaning.

My days as a fan in the bleachers reflect a completely different part of me. During my high school years, it has become a summertime hobby to attend as many games as possible. My reason for attending is never just to watch the game, for I find Wrigley Field to be a great place for

reflection. I always sit in the bleachers, where the fans share my enthusiasm for the experience. Our emotions rise and fall together during the course of the game. On a perfect day, I sit shirtless in the warm sun, observing, reflecting and treasuring. My view is of home plate and the elegant architecture of downtown Chicago out of the corner of my eye. Being an optimist, I continue to have hope that one day the Cubs will win the World Series for the first time since 1908. But even if they never do, I will always feel part of a larger tradition and a coming of age.

✎   ✎   ✎

Essay No. 40

Me? An athlete? No, you must be thinking of my brother. Well, maybe not. Yes, I am a proud, diligent member of Ramapo's winter track team. I drag myself to practice five or six days a week to run and run until my legs burn so much that they feel like they're about to explode. And I can't neglect to mention my ankles right after practice when I can hardly walk, my pounding head, and my so-smelly-don't-even-go-near-them running sneakers.

Now this may appear terrible, and you're probably wondering why I didn't quit months ago. The thing is, I'm not exactly sure either. When I'm sprinting the track or the circle in front of the school and I'm all sweaty and I keep stepping in puddles or sliding on ice, I often ask myself, "Why am I here? What am I doing?" I never come up with an answer, but I keep on running. If someone were to have predicted my future five years ago and told me that I'd be braving the tortures of Track in high school, I would have said, "Yeah, right. I don't think so." This is because I don't have a history of being the most athletically-inclined person. The only sports team that I played on was T-Ball, but I never really loved it, so I didn't go out for the team in third grade.

But now that I'm a runner I usually enjoy it, and I think that I have found my sport. It has taught me how to be a team player, how to focus on goals I set for myself, and how to push myself to the limit when I'm exhausted and discouraged. I'm proud of myself for attending practice every day, working as hard as I am able, and never giving up on the

sport. Believe me, it would be very easy for me to quit, considering that I've never actually won a race. I have come in second, but it's not the same.

I had been feeling a little frustrated because of the lack of medals on my bare trophy wall. So I decided to talk to my coach about it. Being the emotional sap that I am, I started crying before I could even say what I had planned. He told me that when he was in high school, medals weren't exactly showered upon him either. In fact, he didn't win any. But during the summer before his senior year, he trained the hardest he ever had and when he stepped onto the track for his first meet, he won. He kept on winning until the quarterfinals of the 1988 Olympics, which I think is an amazing feat. He also competed against the rough and tough American Gladiators, which is also pretty impressive. He told me that I shouldn't give up because I had improved since the beginning of the season and I had potential. Thank God.

And now that the season is over, I have a better idea why I force myself to go to practice, even on weekends. I have this dream that maybe I will turn out like my coach—I definitely won't compete in the Olympics, but one day I'm going to win. I'm going to be first. And when I look at my now-empty trophy wall, I'm going to smile.

✎   ✎   ✎

Essay No. 41

For my thirteenth birthday I received three juggling cubes. Made of soft patchy cloth and filled with a grainy substance, they were perfectly engineered for quick, slightly inaccurate catches. After fingering them for a few minutes, I decided that, despite my lack of coordination, I would learn to juggle. "It's a process," I thought, "and I am a savant of logic; I can compensate for my physical inadequacies with my logical thought." To celebrate my decision, I tossed one of the balls up with extreme gusto and promptly missed it with equally unmitigated exuberance.

I leafed through the book until I had a sufficient grasp of the principles of juggling. Feeling confident, I picked up the three balls and attempted to apply my knowledge. After several weeks of practice and

hours of intensive analysis, I pinpointed my difficulty: the tendency of the balls to rush abruptly to the ground. I needed something slower. "Scarves," I thought, but subsequent near-catches with a broken lamp proved that a slower object wasn't the answer. In desperation, I dispensed with strategy, and instead began to throw the balls methodically. For the next week, I integrated juggling into my lifestyle. I would wake up, juggle drowsily, shower, dry off while juggling recklessly, juggle while lying in bed, and dream about juggling. My persistence became an obsession; balls danced about my head, cascades soared majestically over head, and swift pins flipped and spun in the corner of my eye.

The aforementioned is the story of how my interest in juggling began. After weeks of intensive practice, I mastered first the rudiments and then the intricacies of juggling. When I could finally execute complicated trick sequences, it was official: juggling was a hobby.

I enjoyed the change of pace, physical instead of intellectual, and the sense of power one feels when gravity is defied. The whizzing, spinning balls become an other-worldly creation; they move and dance in new and exciting ways. Once a dance has been mastered, I move on to another one. Whizz! Spin! I am the creator and the esthete, making and enjoying. Respin and back! The ball explores new territory. The once impossible is simple. Reverse and under! A balls goes through, and is replaced by a bowling pin. Smack! Reality hits suddenly and painfully.

✎   ✎   ✎

Essay No. 42

[This essay responded to a question that asked the applicant to include a photograph of personal significance and explain that significance.]

"Shhuuut uuup!" yells my mother in French from the kitchen. The next moment, my brother is charging at me, eyes ablaze. My instinct is to run, but my escape route is blocked by my sister, who is waiting for me at the end of the hall with a sadistic look on her face. I am trapped. "I surrender!" I cry out. Flanking me like a military escort, brother and sister march me back to my room, where I am left alone—alone with my violin.

Please don't be alarmed. My family is not crazy, nor for that matter am I. The cause of all these extravagant goings-on in our home is the fiddle—more precisely, my slightly eccentric way of practicing it.

I have been playing the violin for twelve years, and for twelve years my family has had to hear me practice thousands of hours. It is quite reasonable to suppose that, after such constant and endless repetition of much the same notes, they might get a bit sensitive to those high-screeching and low-pounding sounds, resonating inside their ears and rattling their nervous systems. But it's not only the sounds that grate on them. Through the years, I have grown accustomed to walking around when I practice. The pieces I play excite in me such feeling, such passion, that I find it hard to stay in one place. My violin practice is, well, peripatetic.

A typical practice session goes something like this: after ambling around my room twenty-five or thirty times, I feel a need to venture outside its walls. So I swing into the hall. At once, my whole body is invaded by a feeling of great exhilaration. Gracefully, I lift the violin to my chin and flourish the bow high in the air. At this moment, I feel myself the equal of Heifetz or Perlman. Then, out of the instrument comes what is possibly the most aggravating sound known to man. In a flash, I am yanked back to reality and my family's nerve endings are set all aquiver.

To fully appreciate the effect of my playing on the others, you have to know that in our house all the main rooms open into the hallway that I have temporarily made my concert hall. Whatever sound is produced in this passage is heard throughout the house, its volume not just undiminished but actually increased, thanks to the hall's acoustics.

The notes I have scratched out are still hovering in the air when, from the kitchen, my mom peremptorily orders me to stop. Lost in the pleasure of playing, I pretend not to hear her. She then screams, which is a cue for my kid brother and sister to mount another of their sound-police assaults. I invariably end up being pushed back to where I started from. But I am never able to stay put, and before long I am launched on my customary circuit once again.

My violinistic vagabondage has so far proven to be incurable, but an incident a few years ago had a powerful tempering effect on it. I was

then (and still am) a novice in the art of living with others harmoniously. I had started to practice, and in due course I had wandered to where my brother was doing his homework. He seemed to be in a state of intense concentration. I said to myself, "He needs to get away from his work for a bit," and so I began to crank out my latest piece. Strange to say, he failed to respond to the intricate meaning of the composition; nor did he seem to appreciate the fact that he was the first one for whom I had ever condescended to play the piece. Already in a bad mood, he didn't bother to ask me to stop playing. Instead, he jumped up from his chair and chased me furiously toward my room. As I prepared in my flight to make a sharp Road Runner turn, I slipped, and a moment later, with a sharp report, my bow snapped in two against the wall. For several seconds I stood staring at the broken halves, in shock. Even my brother let out a gasp. Then I started to panic. What was I going to tell my parents?

Hoping for leniency, I offered up a full confession to them. As punishment, I was made to pay for the broken bow. From that day to this, I have continued to annoy my family with my peripatetic practicing, but if anyone so much as raises his or her voice in complaint, into my room I promptly go.

For my application, the reason why I've chosen a photo of my violin and me cooped up in my closet is that in my family's eyes the closet is the ideal spot for me to practice. As a final note, and to erase any misconceptions I may have created by what I've said up to now, I ought to state that though I've sometimes used my violin as an instrument of annoyance and retaliation (and I modestly claim to have been quite successful in this department), I most of all use it to express my deepest feelings, whether I'm playing classical music, jazz, even rock'n roll. It is the voice of my truest self.

Essay No. 43

It was early May and the cherry blossoms were in full bloom as the sun shimmered between the passing clouds. Except for a mandatory essay assignment about one of the sights, it was a perfect day for a visit to the nation's capital. What I had not anticipated was a sleek, black memorial

that angled out from the side of a hill. Gazing at the stark granite and the infinite list of names, I could not imagine choosing another sight to write about. So much emotion existed there. I simply had to transcribe those intangible feelings onto paper.

I wasn't very surprised to be included as one of the finalists in the "Best D.C. Essay Contest." I was, however, shocked to win first place in the eighth-grade division. The essay was then passed along to the President of the local VFW post, which was sponsoring a Memorial Day essay contest. Here, too, I won in the eighth-grade division. The awards were purely worldly items: a year's supply of Coca-Cola, a $25 check, and the chance to ride on a float in the City of Greensburg parade.

At the end of the parade, a ceremony followed. I stood up, walked over to the podium, and began:

"A young child rubs off the name of a grandfather seen only in photographs . . ."

I looked up and saw all the eyes on me. The nervous feelings that traveled with me from my seat to the podium were now long gone. The words I had written flowed easily from my mouth. I wanted everyone, even those who had never seen the Memorial, to feel the same sentiments that I had felt. I don't remember people clapping after I finished reading my essay. Maybe they were too moved to make a motion; maybe I was too moved to hear them.

As my family and I were walking back to our car, the VFW President stopped me. He told me that he had served in Vietnam and that some of his friends' names appeared on that wall. He was one of the contest judges, and he had found it difficult to complete reading my composition from behind his tears. He had to give it to his wife to finish. When he concluded his story I replied, "Thank you," but I was completely dumbfounded as to what to say. The idea that he was moved by my simplistic writing made me realize that I was a writer! I had reached into someone's internal self, touched it, and left a mark.

Reading my essay to everyone was one of the most memorable moments in my life. That day I realized something very valuable about the power of the written word—if you place the right words in the right order, you can change people's lives! Despite my many remarks to adults that I was going to be an engineer or scientist, I knew deep down that I

really wanted to continue writing. To remain satisfied, I would have to publish my writings. What good is a powerful statement if it isn't heard or read? The answer was clear: I would become a journalist.

Sometimes I wonder where my road to the future would be leading me if that man had never approached me after my oration that day. I never would have known that someone had listened and cried because of my words. "Memories in Granite" would have been pushed into a manila folder and never have been thought of. The only time I would have even remembered the essay would have been while sipping my refreshing—and free—Coca-Cola.

Now, every time I imagine myself covering a plane crash or writing an article about some new political scandal, I think of that little essay and the lives it affected. I visualize the personal satisfaction of seeing my name in the by-line of the story thousands all over the region are reading. I can only imagine touching people's souls, the way I did that one day Memorial Day.

✎   ✎   ✎

CLEVER AND CREATIVE, WITTY AND WHIMSICAL *(7 Essays)*

Essay No. 44

Oxy 10 with 10% benzoyl peroxide. It was a long name with big words, but I knew it got rid of the dreaded zit. The Oxy mask started one night when I was in the seventh grade, at a hint of the first blemish. I guess I was afraid of not looking the way people had grown used to me looking, like when you get a new haircut. At first I probably used a bottle a month, but with each new pimple I felt the need for a little more of my precious liquid. Within a few months, I was supporting the makers of Oxy 10 on four bottles a week, and before bed I would perform the ritual which created what Doug called "The Oxy Mask." In short, everything but my eyes and lips was thick and white and stiff with Oxy. It was important that the Oxy be applied immediately after I washed my face—twice, in very hot water-for there could be no bacteria or dirt trapped between my sebaceous glands and the protective mask. There

were complications, though. It was critical that my headgear be inserted before the mask dried. Because if it wasn't, when I opened my mouth to put the gear in, the dried mask would crack and large chunks would fall from my face. I don't know what psychological disorder this would be classified under, but I just think of it as growing up.

I don't know if this makes sense, but at each age or stage of life, everything seems so pressing and important, then as you get older and take on a new face, you see that those things weren't really life-and-death matters. The other day my mom told me about something I said when I was five years old. "When I grow up I want to be a football player and a fireman and a doctor, but I don't know if I can be three things. I'll have to miss some football games when there are fires." At five years old it was important to believe I could do and be everything I wanted.

Remember how it felt to read in front of the class? Your name was called, instantly your heart jumped into your throat and your face flushed up, red and itchy. I always wished I had a mask on. When Mr. White, my third grade teacher, said, "Greg, Show and Tell tomorrow," I thought I was going to die. My mom tried to convince me that the class would love to see some Mt. St. Helen's ash in a plastic margarine container. I insisted that I wasn't going to school, even if I had Reggie Jackson to show. She won and there I was, ash in hand, telling the story of the volcano that spewed ashes all over my grandma's house. I honestly don't remember this, and I still swear I didn't say it, but my mother claims that when I got into the car at the end of the day, I asked, "What can I bring to Show and Tell tomorrow?"

Doug just stopped by wanting to make a run to In-n-Out Burger. I told him I couldn't be ready for another ten minutes. "Why?" he asked.

"I'm finishing my college essay."

"Oh, geez, I gotta get started on mine. What are you writing yours about?"

"The Oxy Mask. Remember it?"

✎   ✎   ✎

Essay No. 45

While sitting in the Chemistry 2AP fall term exam, I feel a drop of sweat emerging from a pore on my forehead. God, it's hot in here . . . or maybe

I'm just nervous. I have to concentrate. Self-quiz: poly-atomic ions, dichromate. The drop of sweat begins to roll down my face. When we sweat, our bodies are working to cool down. I remember our recent evaporation lab. When the bonds holding a liquid together break, and the liquid evaporates, the surface the liquid is on cools. So when we sweat, and the sweat evaporates, our skin cools down. Now if only my sweat wasn't water, because water has double hydrogen bonding, causing it to evaporate fairly slowly. And the faster a liquid evaporates the more quickly the surface cools. If only I could sweat hexane . . . if only hexane wasn't a carcinogen. No wonder feverish babies have alcohol rubs rather than hexane rubs. Air conditioning. Now that's what I need right now.

Air conditioning. It's so simple. I remember the day I figured out how it all works. Annie, a friend of mine, was supposed to pick me up at San Francisco International Airport (SFIA), but her car, which I'm sure John Steinbeck would describe as an old jalopy, broke down on the way to the airport. So I was paged. I waited at my gate per the courteous inter-airport operator's instructions, and half an hour later she appeared. And when we emerged from SFIA, a monstrous yellow tow-truck greeted us, at the end of which was attached her 1986 Buick station-wagon.

At the service station, we were informed that not only that all was not well, but that we were actually in big trouble. Annie had been running the air conditioner, which got its air from the air compressor, which was run by a fan belt, but the fan belt was not tight. Somehow, running the air conditioner had royally screwed up the rest of the car. But then my revelation came . . . the service station would not call the air compressor an air compressor unless its function was to compress air.

Which brought me several years back to Chemistry 1 Advanced with Mr. Nelson. To the foolhardy he was Redbeard, to the rest he was Captain Redbeard. No, this wasn't one of those times when on the third try in the lab, my partner, Kevin Pell, and I had managed to make the same mistake. Well, I won't tell you the Captain's reactions to our lab adventures, be- cause, frankly, they're just not suitable for a college essay. This was one of those times I remembered something more than an amusing anecdote: when a compressed gas decompresses it cools. So, when the gas was released from the air compressor into the car's vents it decompressed and got cooler.

The drop of sweat rolls slowly off my chin and falls peacefully to the gym floor. It doesn't do me any good there—if it doesn't evaporate

on me it can't cool me down. But I have to remember: is dichromate two minus or three minus? I can't remember. Another drop of sweat emerges from my forehead. It's two minus; phosphate is three minus. The gym has finally cooled, or maybe my sweat has evaporated and cooled me, or maybe, just maybe, I'm not as nervous and my mind has settled down, and my thoughts have quit bouncing around.

✎   ✎   ✎

Essay No. 46

December 24   Adam Winter

Director of Admissions
Admission Office
Brown University
Box 1876
45 Prospect Street
Providence, RI 02912

Dear Director of Admissions

I did not write this letter. This letter was printed by my computer, as is the attached essay. Since completing your application, I have thought some more about your request to complete my personal statement in my own handwriting. Normally, handwriting is done by hand; however, I use a computer to write a vast majority of my assignments and all of my essays. That caused me to wonder whether the handwriting that you are asking for should be from either my hand or my computer. Additionally, I had to consider the possibility that you simply liked to see handwritten handwriting to make the process more personal and to give the reader a better sense of the applicant. Finally, I determined that my personal statement should be written on the computer so that it is consistent with how I write and who I am; however, my statement should also satisfy the stylistic requirements of the assignment. To

reconcile the two criteria, I chose to teach my computer how to write in my own penmanship. For obvious reasons, teaching a computer to write illegibly was a bit of a challenge. However, I fee that I overcame the challenge and now my computer can write almost as poorly as I do. This letter and the attached essay are the results of my work. Please feel free to compare this handwriting to the handwriting on my personal statement. The following paragraph details how I taught my computer to write in 'Adam.'

I first wrote out every letter in the alphabet, both capital and lowercase, all punctuation, and each digit onto Hewlett-Packard's special extra-white ink-absorbing paper meant for their inkjet printers. Second, I scanned in (took a picture of) each sheet of characters. Then, since all the characters were stored in one vast picture file, I broke up the file into many tiny files containing only one character in each file. After the files were broken up, I used CorelTRACE! to trace each image in a bath process. I needed to trace the images because prior to tracing each image is a bitmap, which is analogous to a photograph in that it cannot change its size without having resolution problems. By tracing an image, the image becomes a set of mathematical equations that can be easily resized by changing one or two constants.

After tracing the characters, came the part that I enjoyed the most. I had scanned before, I had even traced before, but I had never created a font before. To begin my task, I sat down with the user"s manual for CorelDRAW! and read the rules for creating a Truetype font. Although the manual had adequate explanations on how to create the font, I would have given anything for practical experience. The first letter that I did, "A," took me about two hours. I learned may things from that experience including the fact that each line that forms each letter must be welded together, because only one object may be exported. The

experience creating the default character paved the way for the rest of the letters. By the tenth character I reduced the time required to register each character to about 40 seconds. One by one they were all imported, resized, modified, resized again, and then exported to the fledgling font file "Adam." Then, when the font file was complete, I simply loaded my essay and this letter into my word processor, selected this font, and pressed "print."

Sincerely,
Adam Winter

P.S. My signature was also written by my computer. That however, was not written in "Adam," rather is a prototype font inspired by "Adam," entitled "Adam Hieroglyphics."

✎   ✎   ✎

Essay No. 47

[As requested by a particular school, this student asked and answered her own question—one that the admission committee should have asked but didn't. The question was: "What are your favorite places to think?"]

While eating Cheerios, my eyes wandered from the yellow giant cardboard box, to the white plastered ceiling, with shades of dawn in muted colors, and back to my bowl of cereal. I thought of my half-finished dream about a white spotted owl trapped in a fire escape in Manhattan, the wild man in search of purple rain, Zeno's famous paradox of how we will never reach our pre-destined place if we continuously halve our steps, and I thought of. . . .

Taking the M10 bus every morning, I look for my window seat on the left aisle, where yellow sunlight comes and goes, swinging back and forth like an undecided child, as the bus slowly trudges uptown. Much like a scroll of film being pulled open in a dark room, each part of Lower Manhattan comes into view, frame by frame, through my black-rimmed bus window. A frame of a woman dressed in black, hurrying into a small deli around the corner in search of her morning coffee. Another frame—a homeless man stretching his arms above his ruggedly pieced together

quilt. And another, of a child with her hand securely placed inside her mother's, looking at a squirrel as it disappears inside a small garden. As the bus makes its perfunctory stops, I think of writing a story about an old gypsy looking for a silver butterfly wing to complete her spell.

Sitting alongside my mother, I look at the red wall above the my uncle. Walls fascinate me. Walls of Chinese restaurants fascinate me. Somehow I can almost perceive the thin line of residue of grease, oil, and age-old soy sauce lingering on the paint and coating the walls. Small cracks spread around corners, like a gentle pond suddenly disturbed as a stone is tossed in its center, and waves, endless cracks start forming with a life of their own. The wall facing me is decorated with mirrors, dragons and butterflies, juxtaposing one another with a sense of Chi. Beside me, a distant relative of undetermined age leans toward my mother, her bony finger upon her cheek, and she croaks, "You see this wrinkle? See?" Her finger moves toward some spiderish lines at the corner of her eye. "And you say I am 42!" Making a noise with her tongue, she shakes her head at us with an ill-suppressed smile. As the table moves, a four-year-old boy diving underneath, I think of my favorite window seat at the bookstore that overlooks the cemetery. And I wonder about the pigeons that call it home.

✎   ✎   ✎

Essay No. 48

[This essay responded to the following question: "If you could travel to any period of time, past, present, or future, when and where would you travel, and why? "]

The Romanesque building pictured in sepia was the Jamaica town hall, the photograph caption tells me. It also mentions that the town hall stood at the intersection of Parsons Boulevard and Jamaica Avenue. (Jamaica? Not the Caribbean island home of reggae, but a community in the New York City borough of Queens. Reggae is very popular here, though.) I know this site. A McDonald's stands in the hall instead. How strange it is to imagine myself on that corner eighty years ago; trolleys rumbling past me, accompanied by horse-drawn carriages and automobiles on cobblestone streets. Only the cars remain now. Reading a book on the history of Queens is time travel of a sort, engaged in to see what my home was like years before I was born, a mystery as compelling to me as the fate of Amelia Erhart or the extinction of the dinosaurs.

This whole borough is territory that has meaning to me. Another layer lies beneath the modern veneer of Queens, waiting to be uncovered. For example, leafing through my book I find photographs depicting an alien Hillside Avenue. It used to be a tree-lined street with spacious houses; half a century or so later I pass by apartment buildings and stores on my way to the library. And atop a hill in my own neighborhood rests a boulder. Carved into it is the inscription, "This marks the site of the rifle pits of the American troops retreating after the Battle of Long Island, August 4, 1776." I found out that this inscription was wrong. A British garrison was encamped on the summit. The error doesn't diminish its importance to me, however. As a sixth grader, I would ignore this nondescript stone as I readied to fly down the hill on my bike. It waited patiently as I matured, and when I finally realized its significance, the realization was more than an abstract discovery. Because I had seen and touched the stone, it was part of my life.

If I could travel to that past, perhaps I would visit the rest of Queens, such as Jackson Heights as it was being settled. I would go to Flushing to hear Theodore Roosevelt speak from the steps of its town hall (which is still standing, by the way) and read Buster Brown cartoonist Richard F. Outcault's praises of the locale in the *Herald*. Then I would jump ahead in time and attend the two World's Fairs it hosted, and . . . oh, so much to see! This entire region has been my home for 15 years, and I've unearthed only a fraction of the stories it has to tell.

✎　　✎　　✎

Essay No. 49

This is the nightmare that has me waking up horrified at night: IQs, SATs, and, most ominously, GPAs—all numbers intent on viciously pinning me down and making me one of them, like a bad *Twilight Zone* episode.

A faint outline of a four comes through the fog at me. I look around and realize I'm surrounded by numbers—a clan of ones, smoking and clad in leather jackets, look forbiddingly at me with bloodshot little eyes. In the opposite corner sit the fours, smirking and full of superiority; no fog obscures them in their perfectly-pressed polo pants. Taller than the others waft the four-somethings; neon halos blinking "AP" and "Honors"

encircle them as they float effortlessly. In the middle of the large room, skittish-looking punkish numbers clump into small cliques. Lower-twos gravitate toward the punkish ones but still look at the fours with awe. The middle-twos are resigned and yawning, every once in a while letting out a baleful sigh. Borderline two-threes pace nervously, letting out a frantic "I don't care" laugh that is less than convincing. The low- and middle-threes are not very distinguishable; they seem particularly obscured by the fours and toil away noiselessly. Most visible are the borderline three-fours, desperate numbers who grope at the impeccably shined loafers of the fours.

As soon as I enter this mob of numbers, a businesslike three-point-eight rushes over to me. Looking me up and down with a tight half-smile, she finally greets my eyes with a disappointed glance.

"Um, okee-dokey, why don't we find your place, shaall we?" she says, studying a bright pink clipboard. "Okay, Miss Three-Point-Three, if you follow me I'll show you right to your room in the mediocre motel. It's not quite as nice as the superior suites, but then you're not quite superior, are you now?" she purrs.

"No, I think there's been some kind of mistake. My name is Jessica Roake. I'm not a number, I'm a person. I'm just going to leave or wake up or something now."

"Oh, no. You haven't even been debriefed yet, have you? You just can't count on those twos to do anything right. Well, I'm not really good enough to tell you what's happening. I'll go get a four, they really inspire us all," she gushes, moving over to the pride of fours.

A moment later, a bored-looking four strolls over to me, a three-point-eight running behind him with puppy-dog eyes. "All right, what seems to be the problem here?" he sighs, glancing at me quickly before he looks away.

"Look, I just think I've let the pressure get to me a little too much. I am not a number and I don't belong here."

Impatiently grabbing the clipboard from his underling, Mr. Four rolls his eyes. "It is so annoying dealing with you borderliners. Here, see. Threee point threee—that's you. We're all numbers here—me, you, even those . . . those ones over there. The sooner you accept the fact, the happier you'll be."

"What are you talking about . . . that number is me? Oh, God. I've landed in the seventh ring of hell."

"Oh how quaint, a three who can use literary references. Can you pull a rabbit out of your hat, too?" he sneers. "Reaally, this is getting a bit tiresome. I have some calculus homework due next month that I should type up, 'kay?"

"Look. You are going to listen to me right now, you snide little number. Sit down and shut up or I'll rip that body into a one!"

Suddenly, utter silence hits the jumble of numbers and Mr. Four drops to the ground before me. "Well . . . Miss Thr . . . Miss . . . I'll certainly hear your . . . case."

"Thank you." I begin.

"You can't possibly know me when you look at that little printout on your clipboard, sir, because that's just some number that a machine spit out. I have no way of communicating with a machine, showing a machine what's inside me. Does that machine tell you I love to learn? I don't mean I love to get good grades, I mean I love the feeling I get when I write something I can be proud of, when I learn about a period of history when things were completely different but people still had the same thoughts and ideas that I do, when I find a French word that rolls off the tongue like nothing in English and, most of all, when I read something truly incredible. Does that digit tell you I wanted to know about everything even remotely beatnik after I read *On the Road* or that I became so emotionally involved with *One Hundred Years of Solitude* that I cried for days afterward.

"I believe in cities like Los Angeles, San Francisco and New York, where the past is as great as the future and where you can wander the street with bums and poets and businessmen. I believe in beautiful art and music. I believe in the power of theater, films and philosophy. I believe that math is the weapon of the anti-Christ.

"Obviously, I can be quite passionate, or don't you know that already from the blot of ink on that clipboard? I want to go to a college where that passion for learning is encouraged, where I feel that professors don't look at me as a number but as an individual who wants to be an active part in the give-and-take of higher education.

"I admit that I've procrastinated more than once, that I've dismissed busy work as just that, and that I will never be an astrophysicist. And even if I end up at the Marinello School of Beauty, my belief that my intelligence cannot be measured solely by grades won't change. My grades are not me. They are merely small parts of a puzzle that hasn't fit together yet."

Mr. Four-Point taps on my shoulder, snickering.

"Oh please, the puzzle analogy? I have lower-twos who could do better than that," he says snidely.

"Get out of my subconscious, you revolting little nerd," I say, reverting to the cool superiority cut-down used by so many of the threes.

"All right, no need to get mean," he whines. "I think I speak for all of us when I thank our guest for showing us the light. You are indeed not just a three-point-three. What I'm about to say has never been said before, but you have shown me the truth. You're . . . at least a three-point-nine."

✎   ✎   ✎

Essay No. 50

Cars are not alive. That seems like common sense, but it might give my mother a bit of a shock. She knows, of course, that automobiles are not alive, but she might be stunned to hear me admit it. She and I have always had a tacit understanding that we could never mutually acknowledge certain indisputable facts. We have pretended that everyday objects—and some not-so-everyday objects—were alive and sentient. We have invented personalities for these objects and treated them almost as members of the family; any attempt by one of us to breach this understanding invariably would have been greeted by feigned shock and lack of comprehension.

First it was a teddy bear she had taken to college. When I was about six, the bear mysteriously developed a personality and began to speak in a rather high voice. It did not give moral lessons (as one might suspect) but instead displayed a remarkable range of human emotions, notwithstanding minor complications such as its composition of cloth and cotton and the small tag with washing instructions that protruded

from its rear. Of course, my mother and I both knew that stuffed animals could not really speak, and I would occasionally go so far as to ask playfully, "Why are your lips moving, Mom?" But neither of us would dare to admit that a teddy bear was incapable of emotion or speech. She was motivated, I now believe, by a desire to get closer to me by entertaining me. I feared being teased at school if word leaked out that I talked to and listened to a stuffed bear. And deep down inside, at such a young age, I probably held out a fading glimmer of hope that magic and miracles really existed, that fluff could speak if people really wanted it to. I had not yet lost my belief in the power of thought and taken on the jaded, though perhaps scientific, wisdom that there were things in the world beyond humanity's control.

Over the next few years the mysterious, miraculous powers of speech and intelligence spread to a veritable menagerie of other stuffed animals, from an L.L. Bean swan nursing a Velcro-attached cygnet to a snake that had a tendency to curl up on itself and nibble on its own tail. There were numerous other bears, each with its own distinct personality and foibles. Then one day, after my age had rolled over into double digits, adolescence hit me. In an attempt to assert my independence from my parents, I cast off all the stuffed animals and stopped pretending. My mother acted surprised, but I think she had seen it coming. After all, adolescents derive a sense of real power from mindlessly opposing anything and everything linked to their parents. They declare their autonomy through a systematic program of naysaying, and they view small victories—refusing to eat Brussels sprouts or postponing a dental appointment—as conclusive proof that they are indeed free from parental control. In order to establish what I thought was my independence, I deliberately severed a valuable emotional bond with my mother.

One day not too long ago, perhaps three or four years after I had renounced human-to-fluff communication, I noticed that our two cars had begun to develop distinctive personalities. Oddly, though, they only displayed their traits when my mother and I were alone in them. Our Honda Civic was macho (for a car, that is), never fearing momentary barriers like telephone poles. He would never hesitate to jeopardize his health if it would allow us to travel safely. Honda was always friendly, and we were always grateful for his reliability and four-wheel drive.

Lulu, a Subaru named after the Chinese word for green, was boisterous and witty. She had a unique personality that she was not afraid to reveal; on occasion she would even threaten to veer into a large building or other structure if we were not treating her properly. (We tried to unnerve her by warning that we would sell her for parts if she dared harm us.) A few months ago, Honda was totaled when an unlicensed driver in a stolen car lost control while Honda was napping in a parking spot. We grieved (or pretended to do so), and we even set up a small shrine in the kitchen with Honda's license-plate holder and some fragments of his bumper.

On my sixteenth birthday I received my learner's permit and began learning to drive Lulu. I've enjoyed driving, and my mother and I have enjoyed Lulu's company. But I sometimes wonder how Lulu will react when my brother, a stuffed lowland gorilla, turns sixteen.

✎   ✎   ✎

PART 3

PART 3

Advice from the Experts

Perhaps the most valuable admission advice—directly from the decision makers themselves—is provided right here in Part 3. The admission officials who are the subjects of the interviews in Part 3 were asked to comment about

✓ admission essays

✓ in-person interviews

✓ letters of recommendation

✓ the admission process generally

✓ pearls of wisdom about applying for college admission

Considered together, their comments and advice will provide you with a great deal of insight into the admission process and what it is the schools are *really* looking for during admission season. The advice throughout Part 3 will be invaluable to you, regardless of where you are applying for admission. Of course, if you are applying to any one of the specific schools represented here, you will want to pay particular attention to that interview.

Jane Reynolds
Dean of Admission
Amherst College

About Admission Essays . . .

The essay is one of the most important parts of the Amherst application, primarily because it is where applicants are able to reveal the thoughtful side of themselves which only they can speak about. The essay is where the voice of the student is heard most clearly—where the student can say something that only he or she can talk about.

Most college application essay questions are very open-ended, essentially asking: "Who are you?" It is understandable, then, that students in their late teens find answering the essay question a daunting task. What I think helps frame this task is to understand that it is impossible through your essay to reveal your entire life, all of your personality traits, or your deepest thoughts. What you *can* give the reader, however, is a little peek into the unique way you think, relate, or experience life. Talk about something that is meaningful in a clean, efficient, thoughtful way by controlling the scope of the subject matter. For example, there is not a writer in America who can take on the demise of the Soviet Union in the post-Cold-War era in three paragraphs. What you can talk about, however, is your trip to the Soviet Union, or an article you read in the *New York Times* about it, or your reaction to listening to immigrant students on a bus which reflects this much larger issue.

Applicants think we are looking for "specialists" and for students who have been involved in world-changing sorts of activities and that their essay should reflect this. To the contrary, some of the most effective essays talk about things that are quite ordinary in life but are interesting in the way the applicant chooses to pursue the topic and to share his or her observations about an everyday experience. So the events discussed in the essay need not be world shattering; they can be very ordinary events. When we read a thoughtful essay that exhibits curiosity, is well written, and makes us more interested in the way that writer is thinking about the world, then I think that applicant has written a successful essay.

About Letters of Recommendation . . .

It is extremely valuable for us to hear from teachers who have been in the trenches day in and day out with young scholars. A well-written recommendation might tell us how a student pursues knowledge and how he or she manages his or her impatience or disappointment when something doesn't come easily. This is great information for our faculty as to what they can expect from these individuals if they become students at Amherst.

We encourage students to seek out recommenders who will give us a broad range of information about a student. Usually this means obtaining recommendations from both the "quantitative" side (math or science) and the "qualitative" side (humanities or social sciences) of their academic life. Recommendations from counselors can be particularly helpful in the sense that they tend to focus on the student in a more multidimensional way—by showing how the student works in a community as a whole. At Amherst we are admitting people to a 24-hour community which not only demands much of students intellectually and academically but also involves their participation in community life. Counselor recommendations help us to ensure that we admit students who will thrive in that community.

Pearls of Wisdom about Applying for College Admission . . .

Every applicant has made some mistakes along the way—taken the wrong course, performed poorly in a course, or overloaded on extracurriculars. While these mistakes have their consequences, be confident in the choices you have made up to this point in life and in rendering the sum total of those choices to us in the form of an admission application.

I hope that students take themselves seriously in this process and believe that we are taking them seriously. At the same time, students should approach the admission process with a balanced perspective. There are very few decisions that are made between the ages of 16 and 18 which cannot be remedied, improved upon, or changed during the rest of your life.

Theodore O'Neill
Dean of Admission
University of Chicago

About Admission Essays . . .

The essay may well play a larger role at the University of Chicago than at most other schools because we are looking for interesting *thinkers*. A student can be a successful test-taker with strong grades and yet not be an interesting thinker. Our essay questions are quite distinctive; we declare something about the college in our very questions. By the way we ask our questions students realize that their responses will be read closely and carefully. As a result, I think we probably elicit better writing than do other colleges. Most good students write good essays, but more than once in a while we read something in an essay that awakens something in us and that we find very interesting. Many people have told us that they are delighted by our essay questions—that they are excited by them, feel released by them, and that through them they have a sense of what this college is about.

If we read an essay that we really like and that sparks our interest or a teacher recommendation letter that illuminates the student, we may write a responsive note to the student (or teacher). In fact, some of our readers keep a stack of postcards next to them as they read so that they can dash off such notes. A note might tell students (or teachers) how the reader feels about their words, might argue with or expand upon certain points made, or might discuss further a particular book mentioned in the essay (or letter). Sometimes we are so excited about what we read that we cannot help but write a response, and we think that students appreciate the recognition.

The following are some of Chicago's recent sample essay questions:

1. At a crucial point in his career, the African-American writer James Baldwin withdrew to a secluded spot in the Swiss Alps. "There, "he later wrote, "in that absolutely alabaster landscape, armed with two Bessie Smith records and a typewriter, I began to try to recreate the life that I had first known as a child and from which I had spent so many years in flight . . . It was

Bessie Smith, through her tone and her cadence, who helped me to dig back to the way I myself must have spoken . . . and to remember the things I had heard and seen and felt. I had buried them very deep." Inevitably, certain things—songs, household objects, familiar smells—bring us instantly back to some past moment in our lives. Start an essay by describing one such thing and see where it takes you.

2. Pick a story of local, national, or international importance from the front page of any newspaper. Identify your source and give the date the article appeared. Then use your sense of humor, sense of outrage, sense of justice—or just plain good sense—to explain why the story engages your attention.

3. Modern improvisational comedy originated in Hyde Park on the campus of the University of Chicago with the Compass Players. Some of the Players went on to form the Second City comedy troupe, precursor to the Saturday Night Live show on TV. With this essay option we invite you to test your own improvisational powers by putting together a story, play, or dialogue that meets all of the following requirements.

   (1) You must begin with the sentence, "Many years later, he remembered his first experience with ice."

   (2) All five senses—sight, hearing, taste, touch and smell—have to figure in the plot.

   (3) You have to mention the University of Chicago, but please, no accounts of an erstwhile high school student applying to the University—this is fiction, not autobiography.

   (4) These items must be included: a new pair of socks, a historical landmark, a spork (the combination of spoon and fork frequently seen among airline flatware), a domesticated animal, and the complete works of William Shakespeare.

Have fun, and try to keep your brilliance and wit to three pages max.

About In-Person Interviews . . .

At the University of Chicago, we do recommend interviews, and we use interviews to help us evaluate the applicant. We don't require them because we cannot accommodate all interview requests. However, we interview and talk at great length to as many of our applicants as possible. Toward this end, in addition to conducting interviews here, we rely on the 1,800 members of our Alumni School Committee to conduct interviews around the world. Although our interviews are evaluative, they are relaxed and informal. Most students perform very well in the interview.

As with the essay, the purpose of our interviews is to help us hear the student's voice, which offers the sound of the student's thoughts. At Chicago, our classes are conducted almost solely in a seminar setting in which the student is expected to speak up in class; this is a major part of the student's responsibility here. The interviews can provide us with a sense of how students think and what they will be like in a classroom setting. We don't ask questions to which there is only one correct answer or questions that are designed to stump the student. Instead, we ask questions that are meant to stimulate natural and comfortable responses. We want students to speak, for example, about their ideas, what they read, what excites them, and how they relate to fellow students.

About Letters of Recommendation . . .

We believe that we are admitting students for the benefit of our faculty; the faculty are in a sense our bosses, and we try to please them with our selections. Therefore, it is of crucial importance to hear from a student's teachers. We want to be able to gauge a student's willingness to share, ability to write papers, generosity toward classmates, and capacity to be excited by ideas. It is from the student's teachers that we can best learn all of this. The more we hear from a teacher, and the more teachers we hear from, the better our decision. Some letters are, of course, more useful than others; some teachers don't have a lot of time to devote to writing recommendations. Letters from counselors are also helpful, but in a different way. From counselors we learn about the student's citizenship and role within the school community.

About the Admission Process Generally . . .

Chicago received about 5,500 applications last year. We don't use the Common Application. Our pool of applicants is self-selected, and applications really are tailor-written for us. We read each application at least twice. Disputed cases and difficult cases are read more than twice. Some, but not all, of these files go to our committee for discussion. All applications are read by full-time staff. We also offer the entire college faculty the opportunity to read applications, and some faculty members do so. A faculty reading constitutes one of the two initial readings.

Pearls of Wisdom about Applying for College Admission . . .

You can't quickly dash off ten or twelve effective college applications. You can manage, however, to apply in a thoughtful and thorough manner to five or six schools. Think carefully about what you want, and write each application specifically to each particular school. Show your reader that you have an understanding of the size, nature, and location of the specific school. You can legitimately and honestly apply to a diverse group of colleges and think of each one as the right place for you for different reasons. I see many students applying to Chicago who are also applying to colleges as different in size or structure as Michigan and Pomona. That's fine, as long as you don't write essentially the same application for each school. At Chicago, for example, we want to hear students go through the exercise of imagining themselves at our school. Tell us what it is about Chicago that seems to be a match for you, emphasizing characteristics that are unique to Chicago—such as our Core Curriculum.

Treat the project of applying to college as you would any other important task. Do your research, taking advantage of the many available resources—videos, books, and mailings. The more control you take of the process, the less panic you will experience and the more likely you are to achieve a better result. I don't mean "better result" in the sense that you will be admitted to the most selective schools, but rather that the particular schools to which you do apply would be pleased to accept you and would be a good match for you.

Eric J. Furda
Director of Undergraduate Admissions
Columbia University

About Admission Essays . . .

At Columbia, we are looking for independent-minded students who take initiative; accordingly, our essay topics are rather open-ended. We want to give students the opportunity in their essays to talk to us on their own terms so that we can see what types of choices they make—in the topics they choose for their essay as well as the style in which they approach the subject matter.

I also try to learn through applicants' essays something about their personality, character, and what is important to them as individuals. How might you as an applicant convey this? Before you begin to write your essay, reach down to the base of your feelings and try to figure out what is essential that we should know about you and that we might not learn from other areas of your application. Think of what it is you want to tell us, then think of certain events in your life or about people or influences that you can talk about that demonstrate what you want to communicate.

My own college application essay might serve as a useful illustration of this point. I wrote about seeing the statue of Michelangelo's *David* during a trip to Florence, Italy. Up to that point in my life, I hadn't seen any art that really influenced me; I grew up in a rural area without many opportunities to view masterpieces of fine art. I saw in the statue of *David* his conflicting feelings of determination and fear. Upon returning to New York, I thought about that in relation to my stage of life, and I saw an analogy: I was determined and ready to take on the challenges of college but I was also scared of the unknown. I wrote about other instances in my life when I was willing to take on tremendous challenges and learned from my successes and failures (yes, it is all right to admit you are human in this process). Just to be able to communicate that in my essay was helpful for me. Quite honestly, though, I didn't write it very well.

If you have trouble getting started with your essay, try writing in stream of consciousness for a while and see what you produce. You might find it helpful to write an informal letter to a friend who you

haven't spoken to in the last few years. Try to catch this friend up on your life.

In terms of style, don't worry if writing is not your strongest ability. A student whose SAT verbal score or classroom writing is not at a high level may nevertheless have a lot to say and can say it quite effectively in a manner that is comfortable, given his or her writing level. On the other hand, when I read an English recommendation that describes an applicant as the best writer ever to come through that high school, I will read the essay with an expectation that I will be seeing some powerful writing. So if you are a very good writer, show us the power of the pen.

The applicant pool for our Engineering School is separate and distinct from the pool for our College. Essays by engineering students are typically geared toward experiences in the sciences. Many involve a problem-solving theme. Some are about first exhilarating moments in which the student learned how to manipulate technology in a new and different way. In any event, essays by Engineering School applicants tend to be quite different in content and focus.

Do not overlook the "short answer" questions which are very informative during the review process. The "Why our College?" question is a way for the admissions office to determine if the applicant really has an understanding of why our institution is an appropriate choice. Understanding the culture of a college and being able to communicate why you want to be there is essential in making a proper college choice.

The essay is a wonderful opportunity for students to be true to themselves and true to their own voice. I don't want them to talk to a particular audience. I think they have to be in tune with themselves rather than with the audience to whom they are writing. When I read an application, the essay is the last piece of information I read. I want the student's voice to be the last thing to resonate in my mind. Also, questions which are straightforward and do not require essay style writing are very revealing—for example, "What books have you enjoyed during the last year?" or "List the newspapers and magazines you read regularly."

About Letters of Recommendation . . .

We look for common themes, or consistencies, as well as inconsistencies among the various parts of the application. Recommendation letters can

be of great assistance to us in this regard. Assume, for example, that a teacher tells us: "While all of this student's other subjects were coming easy to her, she struggled in my classroom, allowing me to get to know her in the context of needing to work extra-hard." The student might provide us with some consistency by writing: "This is the one teacher who opened my eyes to the world" or ". . . with whom I made a special connection."

For students at large schools, counselor recommendations might not be detailed enough to fully describe the student. In this situation, the student might consider submitting an additional letter written by an employer, extracurricular teacher, or some other adult outside of the school community who knows the student well and in a different context. We require a mathematics recommendation for engineering students, and typically the second letter we receive for these students is from a science teacher.

About In-Person Interviews . . .

We were able to interview 6,000 students last year out of an applicant pool of around 13,000, considering both the College and the Engineering School. Because we can only interview half of the applicants, it will not (on its own) be the reason for being admitted or not being admitted. Nevertheless, interviews are evaluative and informative, providing students with another medium to express their ideas.

About the Admission Process Generally . . .

At Columbia we must evaluate a great deal of information in a short period of time—over 13,000 applications from November to May. Usually, each file receives two evaluations, at least one of which is from an admission officer. About 65 percent of the files then go to a committee comprised of a senior admission officer, the admission officer responsible for that geographic area, and either an additional admission officer or in some cases another member of the University community. In particular cases, we may ask a faculty member in some specialty area—perhaps a particular area of science, or in fine arts, film, or photography—for his or her input on supplementary materials submitted.

In addition, students who have worked in this office for three to four years are sometimes rewarded by adding their insight in particular cases.

Pearls of Wisdom about Applying for College Admission . . .

If you finish your application to a college but are not satisfied that you communicated the information that you wanted to get across so that an admission committee can make an informed decision about your candidacy, consider making those final points by adding a note to your application. You might also consider getting another recommendation that will cover those points. Be judicious, though! Direct an admission officer's attention to the details you want to get across by being efficient with your words and application materials.

In selecting a school, try to match your personal qualities with the institution's qualities. "Priorities" is an important word to focus on. Ask yourself what is important, what your basis of selection is, and why. Ask yourself how the school's environment will accommodate *your* priorities and interests. Also, think back on the many changes that have occurred from your freshman year of high school to the present. Realize that many more changes will occur during your four years of college. Think about how and in what directions you would like to grow and how the particular school's environment can foster that growth. Learn about the school and try to answer the question: "If this is who I am and this (in general terms) is what I hope to accomplish, how can this college help me along life's path?"

Christoph Guttentag
Director of Undergraduate Admissions
Duke University

About Admission Essays . . .

The essay portion of the application generally will not "make or break" an applicant's chances of admission. In fact, the best essays are generally written by students who would have been admitted even without great essays. I don't want to understate the importance of the essay, however. An outstanding

essay will indeed help a "borderline" applicant to gain admission, while a poor essay will hurt a borderline student's chances of admission.

Most great essays are personal reflections—that is, they convey both the applicant's personal thoughts and feelings about a topic. Personal reflection can be quite difficult to express in writing. It is essential, however, to make the effort and to respond emotionally as well as intellectually to the subject. Take advantage of the fact that there is no time limit in writing the college application essay—begin several months before the application deadlines so that you can reflect on what you are writing.

People generally write best when writing about topics that are of personal interest or that have real personal meaning. Thus, where you are offered a choice of topics, decide for yourself what to write about, based upon what is personally meaningful and interesting to you. Be careful not to allow your parents or others determine the subject of your essay. Take full advantage of any opportunity to choose your own essay topic. Most colleges allow applicants a great deal of flexibility as to the subject of the essay. The Common Application, which allows the applicant to submit one single essay to multiple schools, is a great vehicle for discussing topics of personal significance and for providing the reader a "window" into your personality and individuality.

Many students mistakenly think that a great essay must be about some topic or event that would be fascinating or compelling to any reader. However, at Duke we look at style just as much as content. In their search for exciting content, applicants often overlook the fact that a well-written essay about a rather "everyday" subject can be far more compelling than a poorly-written essay about a fascinating subject.

A great essay does not have to be a great work of art. Admissions committees understand that the student-writers themselves are works in progress, and so the committees do not expect perfection. In fact, an essay that is too "polished" tends to be counterproductive. Why? An over-edited essay—especially one that has been edited by parents, teachers, or other adults—becomes devoid of passion and feeling, so smooth and polished that the feelings generated by a 17- or 18-year-old are lost in the style. While asking parents or teachers to proofread your essay is fine, admissions committees expect and want to read the writing of a 17- or 18-year-old, not a 45- or 50-year-old. It may be particularly

tempting to obtain too much assistance when responding to essay topics that are meant to challenge the student's intellect and to provoke thought. In these cases, while the readers are looking to see if students have the ability to respond in an intellectually sophisticated way and expect to find some depth in the responses, do not strain to write beyond your own true ability as a 17- or 18-year-old.

It is a mistake to format your essay as though you are writing a term paper. Many students use a standard five-paragraph format—i.e., an introduction which lists three areas, followed by three paragraphs elaborating on these elements, and a conclusion. The problem with this approach is that it is difficult to bring personal meaning to a rigidly-structured essay. Unless the topic is extremely compelling, essays written in this standard format tend to be boring. At worst, such essays suggest that the student lacks the ability to express himself or herself other than within a pre-determined, school-oriented, classroom assignment format. Many successful essays read like long conversations with a good friend, providing real meaningful communication outside of a rigid structure.

About In-Person Interviews . . .

I recommend that all students take advantage of any opportunity for a personal interview. Make every effort to go to the college for an on-campus interview. If this is not possible, try to arrange for an alumni interview in your home town. Keep in mind that colleges will generally not give greater weight to interviews on campus than alumni interviews. Do your homework before an interview. Read the college's publications ahead of time and ask questions that are not easily answered in admissions material. If you have read college guides and want some insight on the social life or culture, by all means ask. However, asking questions just for the sake of asking is a mistake.

An unprepared interviewee suggests to the interviewer a lack of caring, which is perhaps the worst impression you could make. Understand also that the answers you receive from your interviewer reflect just one individual's opinion. Each interviewer is different. I recommend that applicants speak to a lot of people and gather information about the university from many sources. I cannot recommend more highly that students pay a personal visit to the schools that they are considering applying to, whether

or not an on-campus evaluative interview is available. A lot of information that might be crucial to your decision about which college to attend can be obtained only through a personal visit.

About Letters of Recommendation . . .

We place a great deal of weight on letters of recommendation; in fact, they are perhaps the most important factor in determining who is admitted among similarly-qualified applicants. Recommendation letters provide us with input similar to that of the essay—how well a student thinks, the student's attitude toward learning, and the extent to which the student uses his or her potential—but from a different perspective. Letters that go beyond just character to actually illuminate the essence of a student are the most helpful.

Recommendation letters also illuminate aspects of the student's relationships with his or her peers and tell us about the impact the student has made in school. This is critical information, since in admitting a class of students a college is not simply awarding the students' high school accomplishments but rather building a community. The character of the members of that community is very important to the college, which wants students who are not only going to be good collegiate citizens but who will take advantage of opportunities provided. Colleges look for more than a "match" between the college and the student; they look also for those who will best take advantage of the unique opportunities offered at that particular institution. Letters of recommendation, then, are essential and irreplaceable.

Pearls of Wisdom about Applying for College Admission . . .

Try very hard just to be yourself in the application. We realize that this is difficult for high school students to do since they are in the midst of a period of self-discovery and are still figuring out who they are. Nevertheless, to the extent that you are developing a sense of your identity, try to be courageous and express yourself honestly.

Begin the application process early. The number of applications that we receive during the two weeks immediately preceding our deadline is astonishingly high. Applications submitted just before the deadline usually appear to have been hurriedly completed and assembled

and are generally not as good as those in which the applicants started early and invested considerable time, thought, and effort.

The notion that there is one perfect or best college for you is just not true. Apply to several colleges—perhaps five to seven—that have different levels of selectivity but any of which would be a good "match" for you. If you've done well during your high school years and are applying to selective colleges, then as long as you make a conscientious effort in the application process and trust your own judgment, you will end up at a great school and will have tremendous opportunities. You may not end up at the school that at the time you applied was your first choice, but most of us in life don't end up with our first choice in most matters. Life is about playing the hand you were dealt and doing as well as you can with that hand.

Vince Cuseo
Senior Associate Dean of Admission
Grinnell College

About Admission Essays . . .

Since the Common Application has become more widespread, it is more important than ever to read the essay questions asked by schools that don't use the Common Application carefully and to answer the question specifically. If you intend on submitting your Common Application essay in response to the institutional essay topic, be certain to tailor your answer to fit the school's question. No one wants a "retread" essay. Another mistake occurs when students try to take on too much in their essay and, as a result, are too general in responding to the question. Focus on something about which you are passionate, something that moves you. That energy will translate onto paper. Your essay will provide the reader with a third dimension of you.

There is so much anxiety about the essay because it is the only part of the application over which students have complete control. Be yourself. The danger is that students can acquire so much advice from books, parents, peers, and teachers that by the time they submit their essay it is no longer their own; it loses its immediacy. There is a fine line between

receiving good advice and receiving so much advice that it prevents you from revealing in your essay something that distinguishes you.

Good writers generally make numerous revisions to their drafts. Don't begin the process one evening and expect to produce an essay that you are going to be completely comfortable with that same night. A good essay takes time to write. In addition, good writing is concise writing. Try to restrict your essay answers to the space provided by the school or within the word limitations recommended.

About In-Person Interviews . . .

Grinnell is a small college that strongly recommends but does not require an interview. Our interviews are evaluative as well as informational. After the interview, a write-up goes into the student's file; so the session does have a bearing on the process. As at most colleges, however, rarely is the interview or the essay the defining factor in our admission decision.

The prospect of an interview often elicits high anxiety for students because they are on their own, one-on-one with an alumnus or an admission officer. An interview can hurt you only if you approach it ill-prepared and with no sense of what goes on during an interview. Prepare for your interview by anticipating the areas of discussion: your passions, your favorite class or teacher, your activities outside of class, and so forth. However, be sure you answer the questions that you are asked rather than reciting prepared or "canned" responses. Try to approach the interview as an opportunity for self-discovery and self-reflection.

Do some research on a school before your interview, even if the research involves merely reading the school's general information catalog. Read carefully the particular college's instructions regarding the interview process. Prepare particular questions pertaining to that school. Also, go into the interview with a good idea why you may want to attend that particular school. A student interviewing at Grinnell, for example, might be attracted to our open curriculum and wish to focus on that feature during the interview.

About Letters of Recommendation . . .

Beyond the information they provide about a student's intellectual skills, teacher assessments are quite helpful to us as a residential college since we look for applicants with interpersonal skills and with tolerance of differences. We want frank evaluations from teachers. Unfortunately, teacher recommendations are becoming less candid. There is greater pressure these days for teachers and counselors to present the student only in the "best" light. We prefer frank critiques. Teachers should try to provide details and anecdotal information about the student and try to avoid generalities and attempts to distinguish among top students. Comparative information is particularly helpful. We find quite helpful answers to questions such as: What is the applicant's place in class relative to others? Is the applicant more vocal than his or her classmates? More opinionated? Shyer?

Students should choose their teacher recommenders wisely. Select teachers who know you well and can write anecdotally, adding a critical third dimension. If you plan to ask a teacher from your junior year, request a letter of recommendation at the tail end of your tenure together. That way, the recommendation is fresh. Your junior-year teachers will probably be flattered and appreciative that you requested a recommendation so far in advance.

About the Admission Process Generally . . .

At Grinnell, we review about 2,200 applications each year for 380 places, using a relatively scientific process driven by an internal rating system to select from that pool. Everyone on our staff reads applications. Under our rating system, about 40% of the files will get a second "read," while the other 60% of the applicants are either immediately admitted or denied. After a second read, about 300 files are sent to our Admission Board, which is composed of myself, the director, and three faculty members. Staff members do not participate at this point. The percentage of applicants to Grinnell who are admitted is fairly high, but the quality of the applicant pool is unusually strong. Our applicants tend to "self-select" Grinnell and are familiar with its academic demands.

Pearls of Wisdom about Applying for College Admission . . .

The college admission process forces a student, probably for the first time, to be self-reflective. The admission process can be exciting because of the self-discovery and self-exploration it requires. You are provided with an opportunity to think carefully about yourself and to assess who you are and what you think you are becoming. Self-assessment and self-discovery are not easy, however. Recognize that this process is going to take time. Approach the admission process not as a hurdle but rather as an opportunity to learn about yourself.

Think of applying to college as though you are taking another class. Carve out time on a weekly basis to work on researching and applying to colleges. To relieve any anxiety you may be experiencing, you should remind yourself that you will most likely be attending a college the following fall that you will fully enjoy. While colleges do have distinguishing characteristics, there are many similarities among them. There is no one particular school that is the only match for a student; rather, there are multiple colleges at which a student would be fulfilled .

Try to be supportive of your classmates during the admission process. If you support your peers and be yourself, you won't wind up damaging personal relationships you have developed throughout your high school experience. Don't perceive classmates as competitors and disrupt the personal bonds that are meaningful to you. Also, recognize that your family dynamics will probably change during the admission process. Parents and siblings will begin to experience separation anxiety. Remember, you're all in this together; support one another.

Richard Avitabile
Vice Provost Enrollment Services & Planning
New York University

About Admission Essays . . .

We receive many applications and do not have an opportunity to meet every one of the applicants who applies for our freshman class. As a result, we think that personal comments, both from recommenders and from the applicants themselves, are extremely important. We feel that the

personal qualities that come forth in students' comments on the essays and from recommendations are invaluable. The essay plays a particularly key role, not only in selection for the freshman class but also in reviewing candidates for scholarships and other honors programs.

In writing your essay, be yourself. If you are not normally a comedian, don't try to be a comedian in your essay. Tell us who you are, and represent yourself well. Let your essay be your own. That doesn't mean that others shouldn't give you suggestions. Ask others to read your work, but be sure that your essay is written in your own voice and is substantially your own work. Don't leave the essay until the last minute. It is an important part of the process and probably the most difficult portion of the application.

About Letters of Recommendation . . .

In admissions, we are trying to consider not just a transcript but a person. We are interested in what kind of student is applying and what role that student plays in his or her community, church, religious organization, or school. The reality is, though, that we have paper in front of us to translate this information. Comments from educators or others who have known a student in other contexts can help us "see" the student on paper and therefore become very important in our assessment.

Helpful recommendations highlight characteristics about a student or validate information about the student provided elsewhere in the application. Good recommendations answer the following questions: What kind of class citizen is the student? How does the student relate to others in the class? What intellectual capacity does the applicant possess? How do they lead or follow? Recommendations can also effectively speak to weaknesses.

About In-Person Interviews . . .

NYU does not conduct interviews; we don't use interviews as evaluative tools. We do, however, conduct small group sessions in which high school students can visit the campus, speak with a current student and an admissions representative, and take a tour. In group sessions, students and parents can ask questions and can also benefit from other participants' questions that they may not have thought about. The

information session also provides a way for parents to be involved in the admissions process in a way that is not overwhelming for the student.

While small group sessions provide the best opportunities for students to obtain information about the university, NYU also works with alumni in the admissions process to meet students at college nights and college fairs across the country. Even if a school does not offer interviews, attend their functions and let admissions representatives or alumni know of your interest. If you have never come up to a college fair table, attended a reception in your hometown, or visited the campus, the admissions committee cannot be assured of your level of interest in their school. Make it clear that you want to attend.

About the Admission Process Generally . . .

NYU receives approximately 20,000 applications each year. We are trying to help students to find a way to create an application that represents them well and allows them to be in greater control of the process. Applicants to NYU are not required to use our own form but must use a form that replicates ours fairly closely. We encourage students to use the Common Application, and we will accept applications generated by the College Board's ExPAN System as well as by several other proprietary vendors.

Each of our schools—arts and sciences, business, education, performance, and so forth—has its own admissions committee. As a result, applications to an NYU school are read by one of our admissions staff member and sometimes by someone from the committee that represents that school. The first reader is always an admissions staff member. Second readers may be either a senior member of our admissions staff or a faculty member or other representative of the school to which the applicant is applying. In performance programs, for example, second readers are those who have conducted auditions or reviewed the applicant's creative material. In most cases, two readers are sufficient. Applications requiring additional evaluation will be reviewed by a committee. Additional reviews, if necessary, would be handled by the Associate Director or Director of Admission and/or by the associate dean or dean of the school to which the student has applied.

Pearls of Wisdom about Applying for College Admission . . .

Although you may feel that you are out of control as an applicant in the admissions process, there are key elements of the process over which you actually have absolute control. You control which schools you apply to for admission. There are thousands to choose from, and selecting appropriate schools for your needs and talents will maximize your chances of receiving good news in April. What you have done in your secondary-school curriculum is perhaps the greatest source of student control. The element of control here is what you have accomplished; your activities and the grades you have earned are all your doing. Finally, a good, polished essay within a carefully constructed application affords you the opportunity to be present, in a sense, when the committee meets, adding another element of control.

We know that the process is confusing because each school imposes various deadlines. Read every institution's procedural rules for submitting your application, paying special attention not only to admission application deadline but also to financial aid and deposit deadlines. Adhere strictly to these deadlines.

My final bit of advice: Don't send us balloons!

Lee Stetson
Dean of Admissions
University of Pennsylvania

About Admission Essays . . .

So many of the applications submitted to us are from students who possess excellent academic credentials. One way that we distinguish among students is through the essay. The essay provides applicants with the opportunity to become real and fully dimensional to the readers. It also provides a forum for the applicant to come forward about life's priorities; we look at the essay as the culmination of how a student thinks about what is important to him or her.

A student's ability to be introspective and reflective really comes through in the essay and provides meaning to the reader. Look back over your high school years, both inside and outside of school, and attempt to

view this period within the context of the bigger picture and grander scheme of your life. Reflect upon what this period has meant to you within the framework of your life, and ask yourself where you see yourself heading.

About In-Person Interviews . . .

We highly recommend, but do not require, an interview. The interview, like the essay, is one part of the collage of information we review. Penn makes use of a network of over 4,000 alumni nationwide and internationally for conducting interviews.

Our interviews are not heavily evaluative but rather are intended to be informational. In other words, we treat interviews as an information exchange—an opportunity for a prospective applicant to relate to alumni who represent the Penn presence in their home community. After the meeting, a write-up is added to the student's file and may either reiterate what we already know about the applicant or serve to further distinguish the applicant.

About Letters of Recommendation . . .

Recommendations provide us with a broader perspective of the student and a different perspective from the one provided by the essay. School recommendations are the most important. To help us assess the student's academic strengths, we require two faculty letters. We also require one counselor letter, which is intended to serve as a summary or overview. Supplemental letters are also helpful if they come from another venue of the applicant's adolescent experience and can provide a different dimension to a student. A helpful supplemental letter might come from an employer, camp counselor, or group leader.

Pearls of Wisdom about Applying for College Admission . . .

Be reflective in the application process and understand that the admission process comes down to looking for a good match between an applicant and a school. Parents tend to be overly concerned with the "prestige factor"—a school's name. The school's level of prestige is usually not the most important issue in a good match. Parents should serve as a guide

but remember to let the child make his or her own choice. I would urge parents to allow some distance between themselves and their children during this trying time.

Applicants do not need to walk on water to be admitted to Penn. We may see potential for a "Renaissance candidate," but applicants cannot be all things to all people, nor should they try to be.

Joseph Allen
Dean of Admission and Financial Aid and Author of
The 10-Minute Guide to Choosing a College (ARCO)
University of Southern California

About Admission Essays . . .

Your essay should provide the reader with a fuller view of who you are and how you think. You don't need to write about thermonuclear war or a life-shattering event. Everyday happenings in our lives often reveal more about who we are and what makes us tick.

I encourage students to find their "authentic voice"—their true voice from the heart—and express it through their essays. We all have experienced the authentic voice at one time or another, perhaps in particular letters or notes we have written or in conversations we have had—where we somehow found just the right words to express our feelings. You must spend a great deal of time with your essay in order for it to express this authentic voice.

The most memorable application essay I have ever read, in which the applicant expressed how she viewed herself, was so richly textured and layered that I knew that this applicant had labored to present her authentic voice. I had the privilege of meeting this applicant later when she was attending USC, and I asked her about how she composed her essay. It turned out that she came from a very large family, growing up under one roof not only with several brothers and sisters but also with her aunt, uncle, and their children. In writing her college application essay, she decided to take advantage of this "full house." After writing the first draft, she posted it to the refrigerator door, inviting family members and others who visited the kitchen to comment on any part of it. By collecting feedback as to how others viewed her, she was able to

look more deeply inward—to become more introspective. The result was a genuine, richly textured essay authored in the "authentic voice."

About In-Person Interviews . . .

The interview is really a two-way street—while you are asked about yourself, you also have a chance to inquire about the particular institution. Show your interviewer that you have done your homework and have read and learned something about the school. Your question(s) should demonstrate that you are serious about applying to the particular school. Rather than posing general questions already answered in the school's admissions literature and other publications, try to ask thoughtful, pointed questions. A prospective psychology student might ask, for example: "I read that your psychology department is known for its intense clinical program. If I am interested in research and organizational psychology, will my needs be met in your clinically based program as well?" A pre-med applicant might ask: "Is it possible to participate in your overseas programs and complete the pre-med track in four years, or is that unrealistic?"

Dress comfortably and appropriately for the interview, but be yourself. I remember a young man I interviewed who came into my office in a three-piece suit, dripping in perspiration and looking very uncomfortable. I told him to feel free to remove his jacket, and when he did I asked if he had ever worn a suit before. He replied, "No." His new outfit prevented him from being comfortable and being himself.

Pearls of Wisdom about Applying for College Admission . . .

Students try too often to contort their lives to fit what they think we on the admission committees want to see. Many students think there is some perfect picture that they must match in order for us to be interested in them. High school students often ask me questions such as: "If I were to volunteer for the homeless, what would you think about that? Would that help me get in?" However, the question is not what *we* would think of it, but rather what the student believes is important.

In selecting a college, do not allow the rankings that appear in publications such as *U.S. News and World Report* to limit your range of schools to consider. These rankings may not address your own personal

criteria for selecting a college. Look beyond the select few choices at the top of the rankings and the well-known colleges to find those schools that fit your personal needs. Up to this point in your life, your thoughts and actions have been determined largely by the influence of others: your parents, siblings, teachers, and your peer group. Now this is your turn—your time—to decide for yourself what you want. Look inward to assess your own dreams and hopes for college.

James Montoya
Former Dean of Admission and Financial Aid
Stanford University

About Admission Essays . . .

Writing an effective college application essay is not as difficult as many students and parents think. Holly Thompson, Senior Associate Director of Admission at Stanford, has compiled the following advice, which our admission office uses, regarding essay writing:

1. Answer the question; be sure you understand the purpose of the essay and consider your audience.

2. Tell a story.

3. Tell a story only you can tell.

4. Tell it in your own voice.

5. Reflect on the meaning of your story.

6. Write about the specific rather than the general, the concrete rather than the abstract.

7. Don't insult your readers' intelligence either by turning your essay into a "resumé in prose" or by attempting to explain away some shortcoming.

8. Avoid gimmicks of any kind.

9. Don't exceed the suggested length; for most applications about five paragraphs should do it.

Because Stanford does not offer interviews, the essay is of particular importance in the evaluation process as an opportunity to present yourself. In addition to a longer-essay question, we also pose three short-essay questions. All of the essays are important. Significant discrepancies in the quality of writing and thought among the various essays always raise the question as to whether the student's essays were polished by others.

About Letters of Recommendation . . .

Recommendation letters provide us with valuable insight about certain qualities an applicant might possess that may be important to us. Teacher recommendations are particularly helpful to me in assessing a student's intellectual vitality—a quality we seek as we evaluate applications. Teacher recommendations are often helpful to us in assessing personal qualities. Finally, teachers and counselors are often able to assist us in assessing a student's resourcefulness—a quality that is particularly important for Stanford students, given the incredible opportunities available to them. I always take special note of teacher and counselor comments that are Stanford-specific. Accordingly, discuss with your teachers, if possible, why a particular school is of interest to you.

Pearls of Wisdom about Applying for College Admission . . .

Many students make misguided choices in selecting a college. First, students tend to equate prestige with excellence. There is a difference; it is important to look beyond designer labels in choosing a university. Second, college applicants tend to equate small colleges with limited opportunity and large colleges with unlimited opportunities. The fact is that often more opportunities are generally available to undergraduate students at small- and medium-sized institutions like Stanford than at extremely large institutions. Third, all too often students rely on the advice or experience of one friend, one acquaintance, or one tour guide, in selecting a college. Rely on as many sources as possible. Remember that you are an individual whose needs may be met extremely well at an institution that was not a good match for a friend.

Fourth, just as high school seniors hope that admission officials will look beyond simple statistics in evaluating them as applicants, colleges

and universities want applicants to do the same in selecting a college. Statistics can be deceiving. For example, what does student/faculty ratio really tell you? Are all classes characterized by a low ratio, or just certain upper-divisional classes? Finally, do not base your assessment of an institution solely on one department; the vast majority of college students change majors at least twice during their undergraduate career.

Barbara-Jan Wilson
Vice President for University Relations
Wesleyan University

About Admission Essays . . .

The personal statement is a student's chance to talk individually with the admission committee. Your essay should not be written by your brother who went to Harvard or by an English Department chairperson. We want the essay to reflect the student. It is easy for the admission committee to verify that an essay was actually written by a student—we look at the student's English grades, English teacher recommendations, and verbal SAT scores. If the essay is written beautifully and the applicant is a "C" English student with low board scores, then the essay will not be in sync with that student's abilities. The essay should be your own work. If you would like to seek opinions from parents, friends, or teachers, ask them to provide general criticism and feedback, not to rewrite your essay.

I advise students to read the essay question, then go into a room, close the door and answer the question aloud, recording the response on a tape recorder. In transposing a tape-recorded response onto paper, the essay will becomes more "real" than it otherwise would. Also, do not try to be creative if you are not creative. For example, if you are a mathematician, write about math problems. In other words, your writing should reflect your strengths. Don't fall into the trap of trying to be someone that you are not. Finally, don't wait until the last minute to write your essay. On the other hand, don't spend three months writing it. Rather, write a draft and put it aside for a week; then go back and review it, revise it, and send it off to the college.

About In-Person Interviews . . .

Wesleyan doesn't require interviews, but we strongly encourage students to interview. The interview is a way to make the admissions process more personal and to help your application come alive. Some applicants make a better impression in person than on paper. If you don't think you will interview well and that you come across stronger on paper alone, then don't interview.

If you interview with a school, be sure to ask your interviewer whether your meeting is evaluative—i.e., a written evaluation of the interview will be added to your file—or purely informational. Walk into the interview prepared to incorporate or weave into the interview the three most significant things about you. Be sure that one of your topics comments on a personal weakness, if it exists. For example, if you have a bad grade or low SAT score, address that in your interview. Explain these grades and put them in context. The admission committee is going to find out anyway about these weaknesses, so address them up front in your discussion. It is rare that an interview alone will keep you out of an institution, so keep your conversation honest and open.

Don't whine or complain during the interview about your teachers. If you had a bad teacher, keep that to yourself. Blaming a teacher for your performance won't win your interviewer's approval. Prepare some good questions that don't have obvious answers. For example, don't ask questions such as: "How large is the school?" Also, be aware that your interviewer may not be an admissions director or alumnus but may instead be a senior-level student at that university. Take an interview with a student representative just as seriously as you would an interview with a staff member. Wesleyan carefully selects and trains current seniors to be interviewers, and the admission committee highly regards their comments.

About Letters of Recommendation . . .

People who know you well should write your letters of recommendation. The name or title of the person writing your letter (for example, "Department Chair" or "Program Director") is less important than finding a person who really knows you and will take time to write a thoughtful letter on your behalf. A teacher who has worked with you or

has observed your progress through three years of high school is a perfect person to ask for a recommendation letter.

Do not ask friends of friends with high-profile names or positions to write a letter for you in place of obtaining a teacher's recommendation. If you must submit such letters, use them as a supplemental rather than a substantive letter. When you ask teachers to write a letter for you, supply them with a copy of your resume and a writing sample or other work you have done for that teacher. This will spark ideas for them and will help them to write a solid recommendation. Wesleyan requires two recommendation letters—one from a math or science teacher and one from an English or history teacher. For schools that do not specify which disciplines you need letters from, I would encourage applicants to obtain letters from teachers representing diverse curriculum areas. Finally, do not worry about criticisms that a teacher may write. I think letters of recommendation that include critical statements are more believable.

Pearls of Wisdom about Applying for College Admission . . .

Please don't place undue emphasize on how to "package" yourself in applying for admission, Most admissions decisions are based on academic and extracurricular achievement rather than on how the applicant packages himself or herself. You will have fine choices among schools if you took good courses and did well in them. Don't let your academic performance during your senior year suffer as a result of "stressing out" over your college applications. The schools will respond more favorably to you if you did well your senior year than if you spent your entire fall semester worrying solely about applying to colleges or writing the "perfect" essay.

Tom Parker
Director (Dean) of Admission (and Financial Aid)
Williams College (Now at Amherst College)

About Admission Essays . . .

We take the essay very seriously, and so should the applicant. Highly selective schools read every piece of information in a file, includin

essays. While the essay can never be so good that it compensates for everything else in the application, essays are important to us because we make very fine distinctions among applicants.

Once you know that you will apply to a particular school, look very carefully and as early as possible at the school's essay topic. Do not just sit down and write the essay. I believe that the best and most creative ideas emerge not while cramming or forcing an essay onto a computer but rather during a relaxing and mind-clearing activity, such as a bike ride or jog.

Essay topics are designed generally to draw out the student's creativity and thought processes by requiring him or her to assess abstractions as well as to discuss the concrete world. The process of writing a mechanically sound essay is an integral part of this. Some bright students write poor admission essays that demonstrate to us that they are either careless, sloppy, or overly confident—that they are certain their grades and other accomplishments will be enough to get them admitted.

Call the admission office to ask questions about your essay. For example, if there is a word limit that concerns you, feel free to inquire. Don't listen to anyone other than admission officers regarding your essay. Students get terrible advice from adults who mistakenly think they know what they are talking about. For instance, many adults advise students to write about something "extraordinary"; however, most 17-year-olds are too young to have experienced something extraordinary. Focus instead on being genuine and sincere. Don't pretend to be someone you aren't.

About In-Person Interviews . . .

At Williams, interviews are not required and are not evaluative. Although we do write-ups after interviews, they are not evaluative but rather focus solely on "hard" information. For example, a write-up may include comments such as: "Joe attends a tiny high school that does not advanced-placement courses"; "Sarah dropped a course her junior focus on learning to play the guitar"; or "Jimmy quit the soccer ause of an injury." What a student wears to a Williams akes little difference, although some interviewers would be a y sloppiness.

One of the most confusing aspects of the admission process for applicants involves the different policies among the schools regarding interviews. Many colleges indicate that an interview is not required but recommended, but what this statement really means differs from school to school. Call the admission offices to ask about interviews so that you are clear on the policy of each school.

For schools that do conduct evaluative interviews, the days of tough, cut-throat interviews are largely over. Today, the interviewer usually strives for a relaxing conversation with the applicant. This isn't to say that the student should not prepare for the interview. Think about the obvious questions you are going to be asked; be ready to comment on your courses, interests, what you do with your spare time and your summers, and so forth. Read about the school beforehand, as it is inevitable that you will have time to ask questions. Have questions written down prior to your interview, and use them as your security blanket; you won't be judged harshly for doing so.

About Letters of Recommendation . . .

We look at an applicant's file for internal consistency, and more often than not we find it. For example, a high verbal SAT score usually yields a superb essay and strong, glowing recommendations from English teachers. The recommendation can help shed light on internally inconsistent files. In fact, we probably spend more time reviewing the essays and recommendations in these internally inconsistent files than on any other single task. Admission officers are like attorneys in that they must constantly flip back and forth through a file to sort out a puzzle.

Don't wait until the last minute to approach potential recommenders. Give your forms to teachers in October, not December. The holidays put time pressure on your recommenders, and they will not do as good a job for you under such pressure. Spend time talking to your recommender. Ask your teachers if they feel that they know you well enough to write letters in your support. Finally, as a courtesy, give your teachers stamped business envelopes already addressed to the schools.

About the Admission Process Generally . . .

If an applicant can visualize what an admission officer does, it makes the process less daunting. At Williams, a file is read anywhere from two to

four times. Files read only twice are the "easy denies." Most files are read three times, while those in the "gray area" can be read up to four times. Applications are read exclusively by our full-time admission staff. They are read alphabetically and not by region. A file is graded on an academic basis as well as a non-academic basis, and a paragraph is written on each candidate.

Admission officers at competitive colleges such as Williams must struggle to find meaningful distinctions among applicants since so many are qualified and since there are more of them than we can admit. In this struggle, admission officers are looking for reasons to accept rather than reject; that is, they prefer to make distinctions between students based on the positive rather than negative. Accordingly, non-academic successes definitely come into play in most cases. In some cases, submitting poetry, artwork, or a portfolio may benefit the applicant.

In other countries—Germany, France, Great Britain, and Japan, to name a few—the equivalent of our high school system is more uniformly structured than ours. Perhaps the biggest challenge in admissions for us, then, is to deal with the incredible diversity of curricula among high schools across the United States. Judgment comes into play far more for us, which makes our jobs more difficult.

Pearls of Wisdom about Applying for College Admission . . .

Applying to college is like applying for a job. Not all adults get every job for which they apply. Similarly, your goal should not be to get into every college to which you apply. Don't consider a denial a negative judgment on you or as a failure. The reality is simply that there are more candidates than there are spots.

Richard Shaw
Dean of Undergraduate Admissions and
Financial Aid
Yale University

About Admission Essays . . .

Many students wrongly believe that their essay will not be read, and so they make the mistake of not taking the process seriously enough.

However, at Yale, as well as at other selective institutions, admissions committees read every essay with great interest. Accordingly, you should devote a great deal of time and thought to the essay. At the same time, be careful not to become so worried and emotional about approaching the essay that you render yourself dysfunctional in the process. Don't worry about how the reader might be thinking and what the reader would approve or disapprove of; in other words, don't try to second-guess the reader. Rather, approach the essay as if you were expressing yourself to your best friend.

I always remind applicants: "Be yourself. Be authentic." The essay is the only opportunity for applicants to express their ideas about what excites them—academically, in extra-curricular activities, and in life generally. If there were any time during your life for you to "let the cat out of the bag" with regard to your accomplishments and what is important to you, this is it!

Yale's admissions officers are interested in authenticity, creativity, and personal expression. They want to read essays that engage them in a way that allows them to know who you are as a person. We are always concerned about the possibility that students will obtain significant outside help with the essay. In some cases another person—such as a teacher or parent—becomes so involved that the essay becomes that person's essay instead of the student's essay. It is fine for students to seek help with mechanics and grammar. When the helper changes the content and tone of the essay, however, that "helper" may take away from the student's creativity and actually work against the student in the admissions decision.

Another major mistake in essay writing is to list in your essay activities that are already listed elsewhere in the application. Such an essay is of no real value. A better approach would be to refer to what you have accomplished or what is meaningful to you, then take off on that and get below the surface.

Another common mistake is to write one essay and use it for all of the schools to which you are applying. This shortcut is tempting, since the types of essay questions colleges pose tend to be fairly open-ended. However, be sure to respond specifically to essay questions the institution is asking! Understand the parameters of the questions being

asked. Read the questions closely, and don't paste your essay to another question; otherwise, it will be perceived as though you did not read the question carefully.

A final word of caution: Do not try too hard to get the reader's attention. Some applicants engage in alarming essays or activities in an attempt to shake up the committee and to be noticed thereby. Some students try to be "cute" in order to get our attention; a good example would be sending us a helium balloon, hoping that this effort will put the applicant at the "top of the pile." I remember an essay that was written on pink paper in an attempt to attract our attention. Attention-grabbing efforts like these are distracting rather than favorable; in other words, they don't work very well. As I noted earlier, at Yale, as well as at other selective institutions, all essays will be read, so there is no need to resort to gimmicks to get our attention. Applicants with artistic ability may be particularly tempted to use gimmicks. If you have a special talent—art, for example—do not fill up the margins of your essay with doodles. Instead, submit supplemental materials to the school's art department.

About In-Person Interviews . . .

I like to view the interview as a two-way opportunity for students. The interview is similar in concept to the essay—it lets the interviewer get to know who you are up close and personal. For some applicants, the interview can be quite beneficial; for others, it can hurt their chances of admission. By interviewing on campus, a nice dynamic is created; you can get a sense of what a university is about by asking questions of its students. Interview reports are written up by the interviewer, are read by the admissions committee, and become part of the permanent student application file.

How influential is the interview? It is simply one of the pieces of the puzzle—one criterion considered among many. All the pieces of the application collectively make up a story—one student's case. No one part of any file can make or break a student's case. At Yale, although interviews are optional, the vast majority of students participate in them. We offer two types of interviews: on-campus and alumni interviews. Only a small percentage of applicants take part in the on-campus interviews, which are conducted by "senior interviewers" who are

students at the college. The majority of interviews are conducted externally in your community by Yale alumni—8,000 per year around the world. The objective of alumni interviews is the same as that of on-campus interviews; in both cases, the interview is a two-way experience for the interviewer to get to know you and for you to ask questions to get to know the school.

About Letters of Recommendation . . .

Yale admissions officers are very much interested in what a teacher has to say about the student relative to the teacher's total experience—that is, how the student "stacks up" against all of the teacher's students over the years. Students should pick teachers with whom they believe they have the longest relationship and where the classroom dynamic has been positive. The most effective recommendations come from teachers who have had the student in more than one class, especially in different years. For instance, a teacher who had the student in a sophomore-year class as well as a senior-year class typically has established a good relationship with the student, and the period of observation has been longer. A letter from that teacher would probably be quite helpful to the student.

In most cases, students should try to obtain letters from teachers of at least two different types of courses—for example, a science course and a language course. If, however, you are a particularly strong science student, it may be to your advantage to obtain one recommendation from two science teachers—for example, a biology teacher and a chemistry teacher. If you are as strong in math and science but you also took an exciting English literature class, attempt to get both teachers to write on your behalf. Variation among teacher letters will result in varied comments on your thinking, ability to write, ability to analyze, etc., in a variety of academic pursuits. In any event, obtain the best support for your own particular case.

About the Admission Process Generally . . .

Each piece of the application plays a role in the admissions decision. The decision is made once the entire file is reviewed and is based on how all of the pieces of the total application "add up." Any part of the application can make a difference, and if a piece of the application takes a turn from

the general flow of the overall application, the result can be negative. If five percent of an application appears out of sync with the rest of the file, we may cast out that five percent; however, if ten or fifteen percent of the file is inconsistent with the rest of the application, the admissions committee takes a much closer look at this candidate.

Pearls of Wisdom about Applying for College Admission . . .

Realize that there are lots of options in higher education. Don't put all your eggs in one basket. You will have at least two or three good choices if you applied to a range of schools. Most students who do not get into Yale will get into other fine schools that offer equally extraordinary opportunities. Realize that there are many viable and wonderful possible outcomes.

At the outset of this process, step back and take a deep breath. Don't panic. Start early. Begin to conceive your college plans in your junior year. Look at the essay questions for the schools you are applying to as soon as you can. Spend thoughtful time approaching the process so that when you do complete your essay you feel good about it. Notify school officials early if you plan to apply. If you apply with a prepared, calm approach within a reasonable amount of time, then your outcome will be better than if you do a rush job.

Most of all, be yourself. Don't try to package yourself the way somebody else thinks you should. Starting now, think about your hopes and dreams and about who you are. Hopefully, all of this will come through in the way you express yourself to us so that we can determine if you are a good "fit" for Yale.

HAVE YOU WRITTEN A GREAT COLLEGE ADMISSION ESSAY?

Would you like to see it published in the next edition of *Best College Admission Essays*?

If so, submit your essay to the address below. Please include your mailing address and evidence of admission (such as a copy of a letter of acceptance). You will be contacted by mail only if the authors wish to include your essay in the book's next edition.

Send your college admission essay to:

Best College Admission Essays
c/o Peterson's
Thomson Learning
Princeton Pike Corporate Center
2000 Lenox Drive
Lawrenceville, NJ 08648

NOTES

NOTES

NOTES

NOTES

NOTES

NOTES

NOTES

NOTES

NOTES

About The Thomson Corporation and Peterson's

With revenues of US$7.2 billion, The Thomson Corporation (www.thomson.com) is a leading global provider of integrated information solutions for business, education, and professional customers. Its Learning businesses and brands (www.thomsonlearning.com) serve the needs of individuals, learning institutions, and corporations with products and services for both traditional and distributed learning.

Peterson's, part of The Thomson Corporation, is one of the nation's most respected providers of lifelong learning online resources, software, reference guides, and books. The Education Supersite^{SM} at www.petersons.com—the Internet's most heavily traveled education resource—has searchable databases and interactive tools for contacting U.S.-accredited institutions and programs. In addition, Peterson's serves more than 105 million education consumers annually.

For more information, contact Peterson's, 2000 Lenox Drive, Lawrenceville, NJ 08648; 800-338-3282; or find us on the World Wide Web at www.petersons.com/about.

W9-CLL-632

BEST

COLLEGE

ADMISSION

ESSAYS

Second Edition

Mark Alan Stewart
Cynthia C. Muchnick

THOMSON

PETERSON'S

Australia • Canada • Mexico • Singapore • Spain • United Kingdom • United States